At David C Cook, we equip the local church around
the corner and around the globe to make disciples.
Come see how we are working together—go to
www.davidccook.org. Thank you!

DAVID **C** COOK
transforming lives together

What people are saying about …

SAY YES WHEN LIFE SAYS NO

"DeForest 'Buster' Soaries has always inspired me by his ability to balance his political, social, and spiritual leadership roles. What's inspiring is that his priority is always to be a faithful disciple of Jesus. *Say Yes When Life Says No* is a book that continues his witness to the power of God impacting the human condition. I am grateful for his many contributions and his willingness to serve."

—Dr. Tony Evans, president, The Urban
Alternative; senior pastor, Oak Cliff Bible Fellowship

"A national thought leader and one of America's greatest living preachers, in the tradition of Martin Luther King Jr., Howard Thurman, and Samuel Proctor, Dr. Soaries has transformed his gift for delivering rousing inspirational sermons into a life blueprint in this powerful book, all drawn from the reality of God's incomparable YES! A must read."

—Congresswoman Bonnie Watson Coleman

"*Say Yes When Life Says No* shares a fresh perspective on how the blind man in John 9 had to live before he was healed and able to see the life he was living. We all have times in our lives when circumstances blind us, and we cannot see what God has for us. In this book, my friend,

Dr. DeForest 'Buster' Soaries, Jr., takes an uncommon approach and guides us through life moments of judgement, loneliness, uncertainty, and more, that has the ability to impair our perception of life. This book outlines practical principles that we can apply, which position us to have our life's vision miraculously restored. Another timely and life changing book by Dr. Soaries."

—**Dr. Samuel C. Tolbert, Jr.**, president of the National Baptist Convention of America International, Inc.

"So many of us make mistakes and are often paralyzed by our fears of making those same mistakes. So we act blind and are often stuck. This book is a push to 'see' again. It challenges us to believe again, to say yes to what God says and a yes to ourselves and future. It's a must read!"

—**Kierra Sheard**, Gospel artist

"What we seek today, amidst the noise and confusion, is hope … and clarity. Hope, in the form of God's unexpected blessing, and the clarity that confirms to each of us that God's promise is real. DeForest (Buster) Soaries, is a spiritual tattoo artist. And once he brings God's truth to your heart, forget trying to remove it. Take this journey with him, and you will recognize that God is an artist, and you are His masterpiece. A man like Buster will never know the breadth and depth of his impact on so many lives. I gave up removing my tattoo years ago."

—**Richard Watts**, author of *Entitlemania* and *Fables of Fortune*

"There are moments in life when we are told what is not possible, however with the combination our faith in God and inner resilience you can achieve anything. Dr. Soaries has written a masterpiece that provides biblical examples and practical strategies that release the 'yes' in us all. This is a must read for survivors, visionaries, and all those who are determined to make it despite the odds."

—**Bishop Joseph Warren Walker, III**, senior pastor, Mount Zion Baptist Church Nashville; presiding bishop, Full Gospel Baptist Church Fellowship International

"My friend Dr. Soaries has done it again. He has provided us a book that is relevant, practical, encouraging, and motivating."

—**Bishop Reginald T. Jackson**, AME Church

"What do you do when life keeps telling you no? DeForest Soaries answers that question with practical, biblical, and encouraging advice on how to navigate life's ebbs and flows. The Christian church has long held a belief in the power of words—that what comes out of your mouth has a direct correlation on your outlook and position—and Dr. Soaries brings to life the power of mind over matter in his new book. As believers, we know that good isn't always rewarded and evil isn't always punished, but we still have the opportunity to live a fruitful life despite circumstances, unfairness, inequity, and bias. Through biblical insight and personal experiences, Dr. Soaries challenges his readers to say yes even when faced with a no."

—**Thasunda Brown Duckett**, CEO, Consumer Bank, JPMorgan Chase

"What an honor to give an endorsement to Dr. DeForest Soaries on such a phenomenal book. Our forefathers truly blazed a trail for us. Dr. Soaries brings a perspective in this book that we have forgotten about. So many of our forefathers and mothers sang yes when the world we lived in was saying no. Now that we have somewhat arrived, we have to continue to remember from whence we came and help the next generation understand that we have not quite arrived. The struggle is ongoing and the battle is real. When we look at the progress we have made as a people and the historical shoulders we stand on, we can never allow anyone to tell us no. The only way we make yes a continued reality is to unify and stand fast in faith, hope, dreams, and God's powerful Word."

—**Bishop Mark C. Tolbert**, senior pastor of Victorious Life Church; first assistant presiding bishop of the P.A.W.

"In *Say Yes When Life Says No*, Buster Soaries opens the readers' minds to infinite possibilities when one's faith is strong. A gripping tale of one man's journey to overcome adversity by believing in the power of 'yes.' This unique story inspires us to be positive, believe in the higher power, and never give up hope. It combines spirituality with inner strength."

—**Ray Chambers**, ambassador to The World Health Organization for Global Strategy

"This wonderful and inspirational book provides expert spiritual strategies and guidance for surviving the times when life says no to all of us. Powerful biblical references provide messages of faith, hope, and the strength to say yes to life's possibilities. Those who feel alone and afraid will be empowered to turn to Jesus for help and to take the steps necessary to overcome challenges. The deeply personal and uplifting stories throughout will be a blessing to all who read them."

—**Nancy Boyd-Franklin**, Ph.D., distinguished professor, Rutgers University

"This book is truly counseling through inspirational narratives, a captivating motif of Scripture interpretation and personal life lessons. Dr. Soaries shares with us his own life journey of converting challenges into successes, drawing inspiration from John 9. He speaks to the transformative experiences of life, the power of belief in God, and the value of belief in self in the face of adversity. This is a very moving, insightful, and informative book."

—**Anderson J. Franklin**, PhD, Honorable David S. Nelson
Professor of Psychology and Education, Boston College

"Dr. DeForest 'Buster' Soaries Jr. has informed and inspired thousands in the area of money management. He used the wisdom of Scripture and business principles to enlighten and motivate many out of the trap of poverty. Well, he is doing it again! In his new book, *Say Yes When Life Says No*, this brilliant, yet practical church and community leader helps us see the light of possibility when surrounded by apparent darkness. Dr. Soaries leads the reader in how to discover your yes when it seems as if no is all around you. I am convinced that when you finish this volume your response will be yes!"

—**Bishop John R. Bryant**, retired senior bishop;
presiding prelate of the Fourth Episcopal District
of the African Methodist Episcopal Church;
mentor at Payne Seminary's DMin program

"We are living examples of saying 'yes' when life has told us 'no.' We have stayed strong in our faith that if we have a vision, God will give us the provision. And He has never failed us yet!"

—**Ray and Vivian Chew**, Chew Entertainment

"Dr. DeForest Soaries, Jr. has brilliantly penned a powerful and straightforward resolution to the opposing forces in our lives. All of us experience at some point in life what appears to be the ultimate no, but Dr. Soaries encourages us not to settle for what appears to be the last word in our circumstances. We can push back and win with a yes!"

—**Bishop J. Delano Ellis and Dr. Sabrina J. Ellis**, Cleveland, Ohio

"Like DeForest Soaries, many members of my family were part of the Church of God in Christ. Like the songs Soaries heard in the church of his grandparents, I can still hear the saints in Progressive Church of God in Christ in Maywood, Illinois, chanting the word *yes*! As they sang that word, you could sense the meaning behind it. Yes, God can! Yes, God did! Yes, God will! That is the message running through this book. Yes, Jesus restored sight to a man born blind. Yes, Jesus can bring light into life's darkest situations. Yes, this book will be a blessing to those who need to be reminded of the power and grace of God."

—**Marvin A. McMickle**, Ph.D., president of Colgate Rochester Crozer Divinity School

DeFOREST B. SOARIES, JR.

SAY YES WHEN LIFE SAYS NO

DAVID C COOK

transforming lives together

SAY YES WHEN LIFE SAYS NO
Published by David C Cook
4050 Lee Vance Drive
Colorado Springs, CO 80918 U.S.A.

Integrity Music Limited, a Division of David C Cook
Brighton, East Sussex BN1 2RE, England

The graphic circle C logo is a registered trademark of David C Cook.

The website addresses recommended throughout this book are offered as a
resource to you. These websites are not intended in any way to be or imply an
endorsement on the part of David C Cook, nor do we vouch for their content.

LCCN 2019930496
ISBN 978-0-8307-7731-0
eISBN 978-0-8307-7777-8

The Team: Alice Crider, Rachael Stevenson, Kayla Fenstermaker, Susan Murdock
Cover Design: James Hershberger

Printed in the United States of America
First Edition 2019

2 3 4 5 6 7 8 9 10 11

070319

This book is dedicated to the memory of my late father, DeForest B. Soaries, Sr., who taught me to put my faith in God into action on God's behalf.

[The blind man] replied, "Whether he is a sinner or not, I don't know. One thing I do know. I was blind but now I see!"

John 9:25

CONTENTS

PREFACE

As a child I was very close to both my grandmothers. Because my family lived with my maternal grandmother in Montclair, New Jersey, during my childhood years, I was much closer to her as a child than I was my paternal grandmother, who lived in Brooklyn, New York.

Grandma Pinkard, my maternal grandmother, attended the Church of God in Christ (COGIC), a Pentecostal denomination founded in 1897 by Bishop Charles Harrison Mason. Her pastor was Bishop Frederick Douglas Washington followed by Bishop Norman Prescott. She was the official "mother" of the church, which meant she had tremendous influence over the leaders and members of the church.

When my brother and I would visit my grandmother's church, it was strikingly different from the church we attended, where our dad served as pastor. The most apparent difference was the music. In our church we sang hymns precisely as they were in the hymnal. It was almost an unspoken rule that all of us learn how to read music and sing hymns in perfect four-part harmony.

Our church organist and her husband were both graduates of the famed Juilliard in New York. The choirs mostly sang European anthems, with a Negro spiritual sung from time to time. For the most part, though, all the music was strictly classical, European, and in precise alignment with the written score.

But Grandma's COGIC church music was much more inspirational, improvisational, and unscripted. There was no need for hymnals in Grandma's church. It wasn't that her church didn't sing hymns; they sang hymns but much differently than we did. They didn't just *sing* the hymns; they also *translated* them by the way they sang them. The COGIC approach to church music was much more akin to the tradition established by Tommy Dorsey in Chicago in the mid-twentieth century when he was accused of bringing jazz and "worldly music" into the church.

It was the COGIC style of music that gave birth to so many secular artists who got their start by singing in church. The rhythm, the beat, the clapping and swaying embedded in black Pentecostal music made it virtually indistinguishable from secular music in many ways. But there were also praise songs in Grandma's church that were never written anywhere else. These chants were not merely translations of European hymns but rather expressions of faith and affirmations of life's ultimate realities.

There was a spontaneity to the songs we sang at Grandma's church. If you attended one of the church services, you would find that, in the middle of a service, someone would start singing aloud: "He's sweet, I know; He's sweet, I know. Storm clouds may rise; strong winds may blow. I'll tell the world wherever I go that I've found a Savior and He's sweet, I know."

Like Israel's songs that started being sung in Exodus 15 when God delivered them by parting the Red Sea, these types of praise interludes grew out of challenging circumstances and accompanying faith in God. These words offered affirmation for those who had continuous exposure to the bitterness of societal unfairness—but their faith was in a God whose grace, mercy, and promises were so sweet that they mitigated all the physical and social pain and suffering.

The most memorable of these chants, which has now become standard in almost all black church traditions, was the one-word praise song that defiantly said "*Yes!*" Anyone in the church was authorized to start this song or chant. That one word ignited popular participation among a worshipping congregation of maids, butlers, drivers, custodians, beauticians, nurses, waiters, and waitresses—people who had been socially and economically marginalized and defined as second class.

At a very young age, I was able to appreciate the profound power in a people who had endured so much humiliation and pain, singing with hope and clarity: "*Yes!*" Life had said "*No!*" to this entire community, but their faith in God gave them the capacity to respond with a resounding yes. Yes, we will gain our civil rights. Yes, our children will become governors and senators and presidents. The theme for this book was born in that one-word song I first heard at Trinity Temple Church of God in Christ. *Yes!*

Say yes when life says no.

INTRODUCTION

When life says no to you, what could make you say yes?

I was not expecting my life to take a drastic turn. Just before Thanksgiving in 2010, a round of medical tests revealed I had prostate cancer. That diagnosis translated into one great big *no*! After deciding to allow the doctor (actually, the robot the doctor controlled) to remove my prostate, I took my otherwise very healthy body to our local hospital, and my life has never been the same.

After receiving that diagnosis, I started reading John 9 to review the miraculous power of God to heal the sick. I have been familiar with this chapter of the Bible since I was a child. The entire gospel according to John has been one of the books I have regularly reviewed all my life. It is the gospel that makes it clear that Jesus is the Savior of the world—that He existed in the beginning, that He is God become flesh, that He died to pay the penalty for all my sins, and that He rose from the grave.

I love all the Gospels. But in the gospel of John, Jesus turned water into wine (see ch. 2), He introduced the concept of being born again (see ch. 3), He fed thousands of people by expanding a little boy's lunch (see ch. 6), He rescued a woman who was about to be stoned for committing adultery (see ch. 8), He raised Lazarus from the dead (see ch. 11), He washed His disciples' feet (see ch. 13), and He prayed for His disciples (see ch. 17). If you had time to read only one book of the Bible, I would recommend the gospel of John.

The more I engage in conversations with people who have experienced life's many nos, the more it is evident that people need help in finding their yes when their no becomes overwhelming.

A young man recently left an excellent job to take what he thought was a better offer, only to be laid off after two weeks when the company canceled his project. The parents of a twelve-year-old gave up on their child because he was so different from anything they had expected a twelve-year-old to be. The mother wept as she told me she was sorry she ever gave birth.

When your finances have gone past their breaking point and you just can't see your way out of a personal quagmire, when your relationships with your family or friends or church get so strained that you can no longer envision how they can get better, when you can't afford essential medication or healthcare—it seems as if life is saying no to you, and it is difficult to get to the yes side of life. Moving forward can be hard to imagine because you're struggling just to get a grip on your present circumstances.

My passion is to be used by God to inspire and instruct people by teaching them the value and vision of life as revealed in the Bible. This book seeks to share what God did for my life through John 9. And by sharing my testimony, I believe God can change your life.

This book is for three types of people.

1. You're in the middle of dealing with a major no. You may be experiencing problems physically— as I did—or perhaps your struggle is financial, relational, vocational, political, or educational. And it seems insurmountable and undefeatable.

2. You're doing fine, but there is a no on your horizon. You are happy just holding on to what you have. You are not trying to get anywhere new or do anything innovative; you're content with your present status and with trying to stay out of everyone else's way. Complacency! However, if you stay as you are, you will be ill prepared for the moment when life says no. And believe me, it will eventually say no. Nobody is exempt from this experience.

3. You have worked your way through a no, and now you want to keep making progress. You are not driven by greed, but you realize you can still achieve more. And you want to achieve the right way and for the right reasons.

Interestingly, the blind man who is the hero of the story recorded in John 9 fits into all three categories.

Out of my respect for this man whom Jesus healed and out of my gratitude for the example he has given all of us, I no longer call him just "the blind man." Rather, I refer to him as Mr. Blind Man. I wish to be consistent with the respect Jesus showed for this man and the genuine concern He showed for the man's future.

So Mr. Blind Man had been blind for such a long time that he had adapted to blindness. But his blindness also represented a significant no. After his encounter with Jesus, he discovered that he still had to deal with life saying no. That is why he made such an impression on me.

While I was focused on my one physical challenge, Mr. Blind Man taught me so much about my need to commit to a lifestyle of yes ... because the nos never go away.

Mr. Blind Man's significant no in life was his blindness. Blindness may describe one's inability to see, but it is not always a physical ailment. It is as much the inability to see hope. Sometimes people's lives have declined to the point where there's something they want but they cannot see it, even if an opportunity exists right in front of them. But when life says no, that means there is some aspect of life you cannot see.

Some people cannot see (or imagine) their children ever being mature and responsible. So many married couples cannot see their marriage ever being as happy and joyful as it once seemed. Others cannot see their neighborhoods ever being safe. There are even clergy members who believe that God called them to ministry, but they cannot see an opportunity to use their gifts in a productive ministry.

The bad news is that each one of us has a moment or a season or an aspect of our lives in which we are entirely blind—we can't see something positive happening when life has said no.

What about you, my friend? Where has life said no to you? What yes would you like to see in your life? Life has probably said no to you a million times. But I'm guessing there is one big no on your mind that caused you to purchase this book. Life has said no, and you'd love to turn it into a yes. Hold that intention in your heart and mind as you read these pages, because there's good news ahead!

The purpose of this book is to help us shed this attitude of never doing better—of settling for less than God's best—and, instead, dream for ourselves and work to turn our dreams into realities, our blindness into sight, our nos into yeses. My prayer is that God will use Mr. Blind Man to help you as much as God used him to help me.

I was reading John 9 for perhaps "the thousandth time" because I wanted to be inspired once again by the power Jesus displayed when curing a man of his lifelong blindness. Throughout my life I have found that studying the Bible is inspiring and instructive every time.

Studying the Bible is encouraging because it reveals the possibilities life has to offer when you are engaged with God's power. So many stories in the Bible describe human achievement that occurs when our effort is combined with divine power.

Studying the Bible is instructive in how to seek the outcomes God's power can produce. Even when I am reading the Bible purely for inspiration, I almost always receive instructions from God while being inspired by His Word.

MY STORY

That is what happened to me when I read John 9 on this particular occasion. It was the year I had experienced a significant surgery. It was the year I felt life had said no to me. The pain of the operation and the recovery process were overwhelming. My mind could not imagine ever living a normal life again, much less living a joyful and prosperous one.

The years before my surgery had been fantastic! I had been serving a dynamic, progressive, influential, and growing church for twenty years. I had spoken to a million teens as a youth speaker and evangelist. I had helped launch the contemporary gospel music industry as manager to artists including Tramaine Hawkins, BeBe and CeCe Winans, Commissioned, Fred Hammond, and Marvin Sapp. I had served as the first black man to be New Jersey's secretary of state, and I had been appointed twice by the president of the United States—once as an independent director of the Federal Home Loan Bank of New York and then as the first chairman of the United States Election Assistance Commission in Washington, DC. In the same year of my surgery, CNN featured our church's finance ministry, dfree, in a ninety-minute documentary.

I was married to the most Christian woman I had ever met, and I was the father of twin sons who led their high school basketball team to a state championship! I was in excellent physical condition—walking four miles every morning, drinking water and no soda, eating healthy foods, and abstaining from tobacco and alcohol. God had been good to me, and life could not have been better.

Having had this serious physical challenge, I decided to spend time reflecting on the healing power of God.

This experience was not my first challenge with life trying to tell me no. I'd had many previous experiences where I depended on God's power. I had trusted God for help with employment, help with finances, help with relationships, help with enemies, and help with community projects.

But I had never needed to trust God for healing because I had never been sick before—at least not ill enough to require surgery.

Rheumatoid arthritis had afflicted my body when I was twenty-four years old, but it didn't need surgery, and I knew God had taken care of that. My doctor told me I would be crippled and incapable of walking by the time I turned thirty. When I bumped into my doctor at thirty-five years old and he saw I had no trouble walking, he was shocked. I assured him that God had healed me. I shared with him that I not only was walking but also not experiencing pain in my knees, which he thought would have stopped working correctly by that time.

Yes, I'd had some minor skirmishes with physical issues, but cancer is in an entirely different category of illness. As soon as the doctor told me I had cancer, my mind went straight to death. Period. In my mind the word *cancer* was synonymous with *death*! I needed to embrace the fact that my relationship with Jesus included the power to heal my body, or cancer was going to kill me.

I went to John's gospel, remembering that in chapter 9 Jesus revealed His ability to overpower a debilitating physical afflic- tion. I went to that chapter to gain hope as I wore a catheter on my leg and took pain pills every four hours. What happened to me during that time was life changing. I was reading John 9 to see what Jesus could do for me as a Christian, but I ended up hearing God say something different.

I learned what I needed to know and do in order to say yes to life even while the cancer was trying to make me believe life was saying no! I wanted divine power to deliver me to a better set of circumstances. I wanted to hear a yes from God. But what I needed was for God to first hear a yes from me. God wanted me to see what I needed to do to even have access to divine power. God wanted me to retain a yes mind-set even though cancer was telling me no.

Honestly, there was a part of me that had given up on ever getting better. I was hoping Jesus would do it. I knew Jesus could do it, but deep down I did not expect Him to heal me. The no of cancer resonated so loudly in my head that it had penetrated my heart and my spirit. God used John 9 to teach me that as long as I was alive and breathing, there was also a yes left in me. God used John 9 to reveal to me that I should still plan to accomplish something new. And that I should expect my new endeavors to happen, even if physical healing didn't come.

I believe that as long as there is breath in your lungs and blood in your veins, God does not want you to stay stagnant. Each day God wakes us up is another opportunity to improve and to influence others. God will help us do just that. Whenever something happens in our lives that feels, looks, or sounds like a no, God wants us to find our yes and pursue it. The gospel according to John 9 has inspired me to think this way.

EXPAND YOUR VISION

Verse 1 of John 9 says, "As [Jesus] went along, he saw a man blind from birth." Jesus saw a man who was blind, and He healed him, enabling him to see. That is all. There it is! When we say that Jesus can make the blind see, those words are based to a large extent on what Jesus did in John 9. But this book has less to do with optometry than it does with getting to our yes when life says no.

Mr. Blind Man has become my hero. He was born blind. Life had said no to him from the day he took his first breath. But he had so many yes responses in him that he ended his day with the ability to see as a gift from Jesus.

It was this man's willingness to say yes in response to so many nos that changed the way I began responding to my recovery and the rest of my life.

Despite how young I look (smile), I am old enough to remember being denied access to certain restaurants because of the color of my skin. I remember when skin color alone relegated African Americans to a status that was demeaning—a depressing and brutal period. It was a time when life in America seemed to have said no to millions of African Americans. This period is still an influential part of our current experience in this country.

A meeting with a spiritual adviser helped remind me of that reality. The meeting occurred not long after the governor of New Jersey asked me to accept her appointment to serve as New Jersey's thirtieth secretary of state. When the governor invited me to be secretary of state, I sought counsel from the chairman of our deacon board, my top adviser.

He was from Mississippi, and his memories of the obstacles he'd faced while attempting to vote in his home state caused him to break down in tears when he learned that I was being invited to serve in this critical position. He described how he had to pay a fee and take a literacy test to be able to vote as a young man in that Southern state. He implored me to take any opportunity I could get to help improve the circumstances of African Americans. The truth is, we are not far removed from those tough days when denial of the right to vote was a resounding no for black people.

My grandmother used to tell me stories about black people not being allowed to eat at diners between New Jersey and her home state of Virginia when she would travel there for family events. She always ended her story with, "But it won't always be that way."

There was hope. We always expected things to improve. There was also a strategy. Bold visionaries like Dr. Martin Luther King Jr., who had "a dream" in 1963 that his children could live in a country where they could enjoy the rights and opportunities we have today.[1]

My grandmother's generation believed in saying yes even though racial injustice seemed to constantly say no. The difference between that period and our present generation is that too many of us seem incapable of even dreaming. We seem to be stuck in life's no without a vision of how to achieve our yes! "Where there is no vision, the people perish" (Prov. 29:18 KJV). That applies not only to leaders needing a vision for their followers but also to us having a vision for ourselves. My prayer is that this book will help you establish or expand the vision you have for yourself.

Life says no to us. Since the fall in the garden of Eden, life has been a series of nos said to men and women. Neither does God always say yes to us, and we respect His will. But I believe there are many times when a divine yes is available to us, but we leave it on the table because we have not heeded the example of Mr. Blind Man. Turn the page, and let's see what yeses will come to you.

1

THE NO OF BEING BLIND

I stood up in the pulpit at our church to preach one Sunday morning, but when I looked down at my Bible to read my text, I could not understand one word.

The page was a collection of blurred, indiscernible images. Fortunately I was familiar enough with this particular verse that I quoted it from memory as if I were reading it. But it had become evident that I needed help with my sight, and that very afternoon I made an appointment to have my eyes examined. Ever since, I have appreciated my ability to see and have been much more grateful for the gift of sight.

The thought that Mr. Blind Man woke up every morning without sight is overwhelming to me. I was traumatized by my inability to read without the aid of glasses. But eyeglasses would not help Mr. Blind Man—he had never seen the sun rise over the eastern horizon.

He had never seen the twinkle of those stars that children learn to sing about.

One day he had gone to sit at the street corner, as he had done for most of his life, to do what he always did—beg for handouts. Sightless and dark. But by the close of that day, he was able to see the sunset for the first time and watch those twinkling stars come out. At dinner he could begin to recognize the food on his plate, which he had previously been able only to smell, feel, and taste.

No longer would he have to beg for a living! No longer would he be shunned by people who were repulsed by his physical limitations and challenges. What an incredible reversal of fortune for this man!

How did this happen? How could life change so drastically for a man with such a lifelong problem?

Of course, the Sunday school answer is "Jesus." The transformation surely did come through the healing power of God through Jesus. The Lord did for him what He had done for the man sitting by the pool who had been an invalid for thirty-eight years (in John 5) and what He had done for the leper (in Matt. 8). Jesus, led by His compassion, did for this man what no one else could do. He met Mr. Blind Man in a desperate condition and left him in a wholly delivered state.

WHEN JESUS DOESN'T HEAL

However, if we limit our answer to this explanation, we are left with two difficulties. The first is this: many people bring their problems to Jesus, but things don't change. They don't get healed or delivered. We set ourselves up for disappointment and disillusionment when we assume that we receive an instant solution to all our problems as soon as we come to Jesus.

The one issue that is guaranteed to be solved when we come to Jesus to accept Him as our Savior is the problem of sin. While we do not become perfect at the moment of salvation, we are spared from the penalty of sin and freed from the bondage of sin. In other words, sin—which we can define as rebellion against God or defiance of His will and purpose for our lives—no longer controls or characterizes us. Sin is no longer as attractive to us.

But our other problems can persist. The issues of needing a job, being betrayed, having an illness, being the defendant in a frivolous lawsuit, being the victim of fraud, or some other pressing matter may not be resolved right away.

Mr. Blind Man was blessed to miraculously receive his sight on the same day he met Jesus. However, thousands of visually impaired Christians will not receive their sight until after they die and go to heaven. Millions of Christians will not receive healing for their physical infirmities in this life as a result of having faith in Jesus.

If we focus only on Mr. Blind Man's experience, we may get the wrong idea that the healing he received is guaranteed to us, and then we might become disappointed when Jesus does not do that for us.

Healing is an absolute promise for all Christians, but the promise may not be fulfilled until we dwell in eternity.

POSITIONED FOR HEALING

The second problem we create by focusing on only the healing power of Jesus is that we completely ignore what Mr. Blind Man did to facilitate his healing.

For me that has become the life-changing message of this story. By John 9 Jesus' demonstrations of divine power are not unusual. In chapter 2 Jesus turned water into wine. In chapter 6 He turned two small fish and five loaves of bread into a meal for five thousand people, and He walked on water. By John 9 it was well-known that Jesus possessed power and He was willing to use that power to serve the sick and the poor.

What is striking to me about John 9 is that it opens with this: "As [Jesus] went along, he saw a man blind from birth" (v. 1).

The fact that a blind man was on the road before Jesus arrived, situated where Jesus would see him, is what I want to reflect on.

I imagine that Mr. Blind Man arrived at the location of his miracle early on this day, not knowing it was the day he would receive his sight. I want to probe deeply into the role *he* played in this life-changing event.

I believe it all started with what this man felt when he woke up that morning.

He had to believe that something positive existed for him despite the adverse condition of his blindness. This man roused from his sleep, got dressed, and left his house to position himself outside, presumably to beg for charity. The very act of going somewhere beyond the four walls of his home indicates he knew he had an option, and he chose to take the better opportunity.

In so doing, Mr. Blind Man exemplified the behavior of someone who refuses to become a prisoner of circumstances. This was his first yes of the day. He believed there was some opportunity outside his house that far exceeded what was inside. His actions indicate that he had said yes to the belief that there was an opportunity—a possibility—and because he believed in it, he went out to find it.

Our belief dictates our behavior. When we believe something, we behave in a manner that aligns with that belief. It works the other way around as well: our behavior is an indication of our true belief. What we do reveals what we believe.

If we believe we are going to receive a check in the mail, we will open our letter as soon as it arrives. If we think a chair will hold us when we sit, we will sit without even checking to determine whether the chair is stable. If we believe someone can be trusted, we will tell that person our deepest secrets without fear of betrayal. If we think a person cannot be trusted, we will smile and discuss trivial matters but never disclose anything personal and confidential. How we behave reveals what believe.

Likewise, when we believe there is something better that can be possessed or achieved, we will participate in activities that are indicative of that belief. Jesus told a story about a man who found a treasure in a field (see Matt. 13:44). Because this treasure had such value, the man concluded that it made sense to buy the whole field. But first he had to believe the treasure had real value. Of course, Jesus was describing the treasure of salvation and how we respond when we discover that He is the source of our salvation. But as the apostle Paul and his protégé Silas told their jailer, the prerequisite for salvation is belief (see Acts 16:31). That man's belief caused him to buy the entire field.

His behavior was clear evidence of his confidence. There is no reason for us to assume that the man went out that morning with the sole intention of shopping for fields! No, ma'am. No, sir. The man was observant, and he was inclined toward the idea that opportunity could be anywhere.

NOTICE WHAT OTHERS FAIL TO SEE

That is what belief will do. Hope that a new possibility exists hones our observation skills and awareness. We keep our eyes out for it.

I am always amazed by the difference in what people notice about the same situation. It reminds me of a story I once heard told by the late Dr. Fred Sampson, pastor of Tabernacle Missionary Baptist Church in Detroit.

He described a royal cat whose kingdom existed near a vast palace surrounded by water and accessed by only a drawbridge. No cat had ever entered this palace. There were many legends among cats concerning what was in the palace, but no cat could confirm the authenticity of any of the legends.

One day an enterprising young cat managed to time the opening and closing of the drawbridge, cross the bridge, explore the palace, and return to the cat kingdom later that day.

It was such an unprecedented feat that the cat king threw a parade to celebrate the young hero. When the ceremony was over, all the cats anxiously awaited the young cat's description of what was actually inside this palace that had been the subject of generations of intrigue and speculation. The young cat took his place on the parade-viewing stand, poked out his chest, and began to describe with great eloquence his trip into the palace.

After offering a detailed description of his strategy for getting across the bridge and successfully into the castle, he assured the cat crowd that while in the palace he did something that would make all cats—living, dead, and yet unborn—proud!

This young cat said that as soon as he arrived inside the palace, he spotted a mouse running through the main corridor. Upon seeing this mouse, he gave chase down the long main corridor, upstairs through all the bedrooms, under the long dining room table, and outside into the backyard. He proudly announced that he had kept the grand tradition of mouse chases alive by finally catching the rodent and doing to it what all good cats do to mice they catch.

The cat said he had very little time to get back across the bridge, lest he be found in the palace, where he would have certainly received punishment for killing the mouse. But he was proud of what he had done and welcoming of all the praise he was enjoying from the multitude of admiring cats.

While the celebratory spirit was still intense and this conquering cat was the focus of the entire kingdom, an elderly cat was escorted into the VIP area, where the new hero cat was signing autographs and taking pictures with his fans. This old cat was not smiling or celebrating. Instead, this old, seasoned cat had a frown on his wrinkled face, and his head was hanging low as if he had just lost a prize fight. When he came before the young cat, the old cat said this to him: "For generations cats have speculated and even lied about the inside of that palace. We have heard that there are marble floors in this palace. We have heard that there are velvet curtains in this palace. We have heard that there are utensils made of silver and gold in this palace. You are the first cat who could verify for us what is inside. Yet all you bring us is what we already know: that there are mice in the palace and that cats kill mice."

Too many of us possess the mentality of that young cat. We miss the big picture and live without noticing important details. We limit our focus to the familiar while ignoring what is new and the implications of what is new.

If we limit ourselves to what we already have and know, we will not find what is new and unknown. To get beyond whatever has not been delivered to our doorstep, we must commit to seeing the details that surround us every day. That seeing may not happen with our eyes. But like Mr. Blind Man, and unlike Mr. Cat, we see in our spirits that there is more going on than what we can see with our eyes. We must develop our ability to notice what others fail to see.

Your first yes is to acknowledge that the result you are hoping for is possible and that it may very well lie outside the realm of what is familiar to you. If you go on your way—and down new roads—realizing that the possibility you're looking for might just be around this next corner, you'll be much more likely to find it than if you assume nothing will ever change and no new possibilities exist for you.

REACH BEYOND NO

Mr. Blind Man teaches us how to begin the process of reaching beyond our no. The next lesson he teaches us is that we must believe there is a possibility we can possess personally.

We are surrounded by news and images of others who are accomplishing great things and leading winning lives. I often find myself thinking, *Wow, I could never do that.* So often I encounter people who believe that nothing good ever happens for them. I am sure you have heard the secular adage "If it were not for bad luck, I wouldn't have any luck at all." Depression and feelings of failure surround us.

In contrast, Mr. Blind Man seemed to believe that something good might happen to him. If there had been no possibility of that, why would he have gotten out of bed? So he went out to see what good things might come. In so doing, he was teaching us that we must believe there is a better version of our present situation available and we can attain a better position. If we don't believe a possibility exists for things to get better, depression and feelings of failure will surround us too. In fact, one definition of *depression* might be "the belief that nothing can improve."

Saying yes when life said no in my own situation required that I learn the ropes in life and determine which strings to pull. For me this became the works that needed to accompany my faith: "As the body without the spirit it dead, so faith without deeds is dead" (James 2:26).

Sometimes our circumstances are so overwhelming that we become traumatized, and we can come to believe that our trouble and despair may be all that life has to offer. This can be dangerous, since what we believe determines how we behave.

I believe you can increase whatever it is you have. If you have depression, you can increase your depression. If you have anger, you can feed and deepen your anger. Also, if you have joy, you can enlarge your joy. Whatever it is you have, whatever it is you're doing, you can deepen it.

So … what do you want more of?

Dangerous is the person with breath still in his lungs who thinks life is over just because of the challenges he faces. Obnoxious is the person who acts as if she has exhausted all avenues of learning. And arrogant is the one who appears to need no help with anything.

There is always something we can grow into. It doesn't matter what our achievements or capacities are—there is still room for improvement. Bill Gates's wealth doesn't make him complacent. A few years ago, I was impressed to read an article about Microsoft's expansion plans in China. I was surprised that they would still want to grow. It goes to show that even for a large conglomerate, even for one of the wealthiest men in the country, there is another yes opportunity in life.

Mr. Blind Man knew there were still wonderful things for him to learn and wonderful ways for him to grow. You can know that too. The next time you're tempted to think you already are everything you're ever going to become or already have everything you are ever going to get, remember Mr. Blind Man. Though we may not be able to see it, there is something better out there for us. We must get up, dust off the despair, and go *out* if we wish to bump into our next opportunity.

If you look hard enough, you will find a yes opportunity for your family, your faith, and your understanding of Scripture. You will see a yes for your church and your business. You will engage in proactive behavior that positions you to reach up and grab opportunities you may have never seen before.

Mr. Blind Man could have sat at home wallowing in his affliction and bathing in self-pity. After all, he was blind because of no fault of his own. He had done nothing to contribute to his predicament. When we experience self-inflicted trouble, we tend to be angry at ourselves. But when we have done nothing wrong to anyone, it is not unreasonable that we might feel resentment and anger toward everyone. We might even come to lose all desire to be near anyone.

GOD IS OUTSIDE TOO

Notice that John 9:1 says, "As [Jesus] went along." As Jesus was walking down the street with His disciples, He saw Mr. Blind Man.

Jesus too was outside on the street. Don't miss this.

Mr. Blind Man had a hope that caused him to get dressed that morning and go outside to look for what possibility might come. But Jesus was out too, and He was always looking for someone to bless.

I like to think of Jesus rising every morning with the prayer that His Father would show Him how and where and to whom He should pour out love and power. When Jesus walked down that road, He had his eyes wide open, and when He saw this man and knew he had been born blind, He jumped at the opportunity to display the works of God.

Yes, Jesus could've gone to this man's home and healed him. But we don't have any stories in the Gospels about Jesus going uninvited into someone's home and forcing a healing. Instead, we have many stories of Jesus meeting people on the road or being brought inside a home.

God is out there looking for people to display His glory. It's true that He could just drop a blessing on you, but the example in the Gospels seems to be that blessings come to those who believe enough in them to go searching for them. How could you apply that to your life?

Mr. Blind Man didn't let anything keep him from seeking the possibility that something good might come to him. He dressed that morning in apparel he could not see. He didn't care how he looked or how people would perceive him. He was not concerned about what people would say about him. He didn't care that children would point at him. He didn't think of how the weather would turn out that day. He believed that leaving home and going to the streets would give him something he did not already have.

So he stood on his street corner, in that convenient spot, and Jesus saw him and granted him the gift of sight.

GET OUT THERE

Many of us miss our blessings because when we hit a bump in the road or get stuck in a ditch, we lock ourselves inside prisons of self-pity. We don't want to talk to anybody, we don't want to see anybody, and we don't want to learn anything. We incarcerate ourselves.

Sometimes we do so out of pride. Maybe we would rather not have people know the truth about us—that we are broke, are going through a divorce, are suddenly unemployed, had our home foreclosed on, or had our car repossessed. It's much easier and less humiliating to just hide from the world.

That was my first reaction to discovering I had cancer. I didn't want to talk about it. That was a problem, because I couldn't think about anything else. I never felt that cancer was really in my body. The doctors had detected it at such an early stage that I had no physical symptoms. It was tempting to think they were wrong.

Now, it really was there, and had I not had surgery, there is no doubt it would have attacked my body in ways I would definitely have felt. But what did affect my mind was the diagnosis itself. When I received the no of cancer, it defeated my previous state of good health, and it was a serious blow to my thinking. In a sense, cancer had a more significant impact on my mind than it did my body. I felt like locking my door, closing my windows, turning off my phone, and just remaining secluded.

So I understand when I see Christians who stop going to church because of an emotional crisis. But who knows what yes opportunity they could have received had they attended worship and celebrated the goodness of God? Perhaps they would've sat next to a doctor in church or met a missionary who could help them, or perhaps they would sing a song in church that would remind them of God's undying love and faithfulness even through hard times.

When life begins to squeeze us, we often become blinded regarding anything positive and overwhelmed by our circumstances. Our first reaction is to retreat, but God may be saying "Charge!"

I did not have the luxury of shutting down. I had a responsibility to continue leading my congregation. I went to church even when I didn't feel like going. Because I wanted my members to hear the news about my health directly from me, I stood up and announced to the entire church that I had prostate cancer.

What happened next was as surprising as it was amazing. Dozens of men in the church shared with me that they'd had prostate cancer, and they were full of information about what I should expect. Had I remained isolated, God could not have used all those cancer survivors to minister to me. I would not have received a blessing had I stayed home, and neither would those people have had the blessing of ministering to their pastor.

Jesus noticed Mr. Blind Man because he was out there. To get beyond your circumstance and obtain your yes, you have to get out there too. Go somewhere; meet someone; try something different; learn something new. But you will do this only if you believe there is life beyond the no you've experienced.

When you wake up in the morning, you have to think it is for a purpose. Why else would He wake you?

Each day that we are granted new life, we find God at work keeping the sun burning and giving us light, which takes eight minutes to travel the ninety-three million miles to reach us here on Earth. He has galaxies to coordinate and birds to feed. He is busy every morning with divine chores: giving and taking life, keeping the snowcapped mountains cold and the desert land arid. God has to boil the innermost parts of the earth.

God has all this to do, yet He took the time to reach down and shake you and me awake this morning. That is no accident—it is divine purpose.

So how dare we sit around and act as if our lives are over! How dare we bemoan our circumstances! You and I need to get over it! We need to say yes to whatever no life has brought our way. This day is important. This day has purpose. What are we going to do with it?

Wash your face, comb your hair, put on some makeup, iron your clothes, hold your head high, grab some breakfast, and go out and meet somebody. Or go out and read a book or listen to some music or sit in the park. Do something to help yourself instead of acting pitiful. The only time you are genuinely helpless is when your body is underground with a headstone above you. Until that happens, you have to try to be somebody. God filled this day with purpose for you. Now go out and look for it.

NO DOESN'T HAVE TO BE THE LAST WORD

My former boss, civil rights activist Rev. Jesse Jackson, would always tell us that if we fought, we might lose. But if we failed to fight, we were guaranteed to lose. So go out and fight!

When he left his house that morning, Mr. Blind Man was not expecting to meet Jesus. He was not like the woman with the bleeding issue who reached out to touch the hem of Jesus' garment (see Luke 8:43–48) or the centurion who sought out Jesus to request that He heal his servant (see Matt. 8:5–13). There is reason to believe that Mr. Blind Man didn't know much about Jesus at all. But by leaving the private place of his house, he showed that he believed there was a very real chance he could connect with someone who would benefit him. Even if that someone would only put a coin in his hand, he expected to meet someone who would help him in some way.

People knew him as a blind beggar. He had undoubtedly been exposed to mean people. Almost everyone I know has at least one person who dislikes him or her. And some people hate you for no reason at all! One of the first social outcomes of sin entering the human experience was the dislike Cain possessed for his brother, Abel, who had done nothing wrong to him at all (see Gen. 4:1–8). All too often people justify their hatred for others because of the differences that exist between them.

That was one of the perspectives that undergirded Christian slaveholding in seventeenth-, eighteenth-, and nineteenth-century America. As long as white Christians felt morally superior to African slaves, they felt justified in treating them as they would the livestock on their plantations.

Despite the fact that mental illness is a major cause of homelessness, we pass by homeless people and too often blame them for their own difficulties, as if being homeless renders someone morally inferior. One can only imagine how mean people treated Mr. Blind Man.

Mr. Blind Man sat begging. That meant he was a member of the lowest economic class in his community. His clothes were not stylish. No one sits and begs in designer clothing. His hygiene would not have had the benefit of expensive oils or perfumes. His feet may have been without shoes. Passersby may have done what many of us do when we are near such a person on a city street or in a train station—look away and try not to make eye contact.

There were probably those who were so disgusted by his impoverished appearance and unpleasant body odor that they said ugly things to and about him.

Yet Mr. Blind Man braved the scorn. He held on to the possibility that one person might extend kindness to him and bless him, if only in a small way. Little did he know that the One he met this day would be *the* One.

I have friends who once held influential positions but don't any longer. When they were in these positions, they were in high demand by people everywhere. Because of their ability to do things for so many people, they didn't have enough time in a given month to fit everyone on their schedule who demanded some of their time. They received invitations to breakfasts, lunches, dinners, meetings, conferences, retreats, and every other type of gathering by people who posed as their friends.

But as soon as these people were no longer in their prominent positions, they discovered that they were in much less demand. It became obvious that those people had befriended their *status* and not them. Their loss of influence revealed who their real friends were.

Yet when all others fail us, the Lord will not. "There is a friend who sticks closer than a brother," Proverbs 18:24 tells us, and His name is Jesus. Even when there are no visible friends beside us in our moment of need, our Savior is beside us. And He will send His servants to us.

Somehow, without having had any formal instruction, Mr. Blind Man knew to stay close to Jesus long enough to experience His power. He placed himself in a "findable" place every day, always believing that good things could come, and one day his faith was rewarded in a way beyond his wildest dreams.

I have watched so many people come to the church, join the church, and then leave the church because their lives didn't seem to change fast enough. Perhaps they were looking for God to instantly deliver a yes to cancel a nagging no.

I had to learn from Mr. Blind Man that there may be some unpleasantness between my no and my yes. But in the end, Jesus not only would give me the strength to endure the process but also would be there to meet me at the finish line. I didn't know whether He would heal me in this lifetime or not. But I did learn that I had to go out and look for my yes.

When I was thirty, I had painted myself into a corner and I didn't know how to get out. I was deeply disappointed in myself, but I felt stuck. I was giving off the appearance of a reality that was not true. I was driving a luxury car, wearing designer clothes, and making frequent media appearances, but I had no savings account, no insurance, and no investments. I was serving as the pastor of the small church of my childhood, but I had never had any theological training. I had never resolved my graduation status from Rutgers University and had not officially completed my undergraduate degree.

I felt stuck, and I could not see where I was going or how I would get there. I decided to take one course at Fordham University to see whether that might get my life jump-started.

When I went to visit Fordham, I couldn't find the room I needed, so I stopped to ask directions from a man unpacking boxes in the hallway. I ended up talking with this man for an hour!

It turned out he was the chairman of the religious studies department and an Old Testament scholar from Harvard University. After hearing me describe my circumstances and my goals, Dr. Byron Shafer convinced me to enroll as a full-time student at Fordham and to major in religious studies. He became my adviser and academic mentor.

What would've happened if I'd just stayed in bed that day? In a sense, I went into that building blind but hopeful that something good could come. God provided in a way I'd never anticipated, and I left seeing my future. It all started with what I believed.

TURNING YOUR NO INTO A YES

1. What's an example of how you think your situation can never improve?
2. What actions do you take because you believe things will never change? What actions do you

not take because you believe things will never change?

3. How can you emulate Mr. Blind Man and go out, perhaps every day from now on, knowing that you might face some unpleasantness, so you can find the person whom God sends to bring you a yes?

2

THE NO OF BEING LONELY

Many of us have people always around us. Most of us also have access to more people than ever before, by way of friends and followers on social media platforms. Yet many of us find ourselves desperately alone. It seems as if the more we are connected, the more loneliness we experience. Why is that?

Loneliness makes it so much harder when life says no. Having no one with whom we can share our circumstances exacerbates the pain of our troubling situations. Now, simply having people in our lives does not guarantee they will be people we can trust. Just having people in our families does not always mean they will be people who will understand what we are experiencing. Even married couples find themselves wondering how much to share with each other, perhaps thinking that silence will spare the spouse the burden of worry.

We learn that Mr. Blind Man had family nearby (see John 9:18). But when Jesus saw him, he was all alone. No one had come to his house to give him food so he wouldn't have to beg that day. Perhaps there had been no one to escort him to the place where he would sit on the street and beg. No one was there to introduce him to Jesus and His disciples. No one was there to stick up for him when the disciples questioned his moral credentials. No one was with him when he obeyed Jesus and went to the pool of Siloam to wash the mud from his eyes.

Mr. Blind Man was alone.

The day my doctor told me I had cancer, I was alone too. I had gone to the doctor by myself. And after hearing that my test results were positive, I felt more alone than I had ever felt in my life. My faith inspired me to believe that God could heal me of cancer. And my belief in heaven reminded me that even if the disease killed me, I would live forever with God there. Even so, my immediate response to my doctor's news was not "Praise the Lord!" I felt alone.

You need not feel depressed or defeated to feel alone. You can be a fervent believer in God and still feel alone. To be alone simply means you understand that your next few steps, next few decisions, or next series of actions will involve you and only you.

Not only was Mr. Blind Man incapable of seeing; he was also alone.

ALONE BUT NOT LONELY

God created us to be gregarious creatures. We are sociable beings made to live in families and communities. When God made Adam, "the LORD God said, 'It is not good for the man to be alone'" (Gen. 2:18). When we enjoy healthy relationships with other humans, we are more likely to handle life's nos more easily. Healthy relationships and companionships can provide ongoing encouragement and inspiration. When God made Eve, she met the immediate need of protecting Adam from being alone, lest his aloneness grow into loneliness.

Aloneness is a physical reality. But *loneliness* is an emotional state that may or may not include the physical state of being alone. In other words, we can be lonely even when we are not alone. *Alone* describes *what* we are, while *lonely* describes *how* we are feeling.

I sense that Mr. Blind Man was not afflicted with loneliness. By studying him, I was able to learn how to avoid allowing my aloneness to become loneliness.

When life says no, we feel the impact individually. Five thousand people can lose their jobs when a company closes, but each employee suffers the job loss personally. Everyone at a school may have the flu, but each child experiences chills and fever individually. Every church in town may be suffering shrinking attendance and challenged finances, but each pastor feels the impact as if it is happening only to that one church.

In that sense, we feel alone. Intellectually we know that others have the same experience. But that rarely helps when we are reeling from the no that has stopped us in our tracks and put us on our backs.

I knew I was not the only person diagnosed with cancer. After all, I was at the Cancer Institute of New Jersey! There would not be an entire institution that treated cancer patients if I were the only person with the disease. That is a rational observation, but when life says no, the first response is rarely reasonable. And since I was the only husband to Margaret Donna Soaries with cancer, the only father of Malcolm and Martin Soaries with cancer, and the sole pastor of First Baptist Church of Lincoln Gardens with cancer, I felt all alone.

Mr. Blind Man knew that he was not the only blind person in his town, but he also knew that he was alone.

When we are alone and life says no, we ask ourselves thousands of questions. Here were some of mine: How long do I have to live? Whom should I tell, and when should I tell them? What form of treatment should I pursue? Notice that the answer to the second question would determine whether I would allow my aloneness to become loneliness.

When we are alone, we have the power to decide not to let ourselves become lonely. Loneliness functions like a prison—it takes control of our being and defines all our movements and interactions.

We in this nation have witnessed countless tragic events that have involved the outbursts of lonely people. Some time ago, a reclusive criminal spent seventeen years sending home-made bombs that targeted universities, airlines, and a computer store, killing three people and injuring twenty-four others. The FBI branded him the "Unabomber"—shorthand for his early targets: universities and airlines.

Despite an investigation that spanned eight states and involved five hundred agents, the FBI could not solve the case. It wasn't until the bomber's brother provided a tip to law enforcement officials that the FBI was eventually able to find a small cabin in the wilderness of Montana where a troubled "lonely genius," Theodore Kaczynski, sat making his bombs. He was arrested, bringing an end to the Unabomber's reign of terror.[1]

While this is an extreme example, there is a growing population of lonely people who feel disconnected from society and are like ticking time bombs waiting to explode. The causes vary, but they all started out being alone. What they all need is a yes to the no of being lonely.

I was alone but did not want to become lonely. Mr. Blind Man was alone but never became lonely. It's not inevitable that someone who is alone will become lonely. Mr. Blind Man lasted through the day by maintaining a yes to all the nos he faced.

What might Mr. Blind Man have had in his mind to keep him from becoming lonely? He was almost certainly familiar with the Hebrew Bible and may have received encouragement from the words of his religious tradition. Leviticus 19:14 says, "Do not curse the deaf or put a stumbling block in front of the blind, but fear your God. I am the LORD."

According to this Scripture, which Mr. Blind Man had probably learned as a child, God shows an interest in people who are blind. Perhaps this Scripture had been such an encouragement to Mr. Blind Man that he never felt lonely. When you know that God has given promises and instructions that address your situation, you have hope.

Mr. Blind Man had the opportunity to be exposed to a multitude of Scriptures that could have provided encouragement to him while he was alone. Here are some others:

- "The LORD said to him, 'Who gave human beings their mouths? Who makes them deaf or mute? Who gives them sight or makes them blind? Is it not I, the LORD?'" (Ex. 4:11).
- "The LORD gives sight to the blind, the LORD lifts up those who are bowed down, the LORD loves the righteous" (Ps. 146:8).
- "In that day the deaf will hear the words of the scroll, and out of gloom and darkness the eyes of the blind will see" (Isa. 29:18).
- "Then will the eyes of the blind be opened and the ears of the deaf unstopped" (Isa. 35:5).
- "I, the LORD, have called you in righteousness; I will take hold of your hand. I will keep you and will make you to be a covenant for the people and a light for the Gentiles, to open eyes that are blind, to free captives from

prison and to release from the dungeon those who sit in darkness" (Isa. 42:6–7).

- "I will lead the blind by ways they have not known, along unfamiliar paths I will guide them; I will turn the darkness into light before them and make the rough places smooth. These are the things I will do; I will not forsake them" (Isa. 42:16).

YOUR WARRANTY

The Bible functions as a type of warranty in life. If we make a purchase and the item begins to malfunction, the warranty is our assurance the manufacturer will ultimately resolve the problem. The language contained in the warranty document gives us that assurance.

Likewise, the Bible is provided by the Manufacturer of the universe, and it includes the language we need to assure us that our problems get resolved.

Now, some people have taken that to mean that we will never have issues—that after we become Christians, life will always say yes to us. That's simply not so. The fact is that most faithful people among us will experience life saying no. Jesus told His disciples that there would certainly be trouble in life. But He also told them not to fear, because He had overcome the world (see John 16:33)—and with His power and presence, we will also.

Mr. Blind Man motivated me to embrace the words of my warranty and use them to conquer my potential loneliness. Not only did I have the very same Scriptures that Mr. Blind Man had—the Old Testament—but I also had the New Testament.

The Bible spoke directly to me as it appears that his Bible spoke to Mr. Blind Man:

- "Jesus turned and saw her. 'Take heart, daughter,' he said, 'your faith has healed you.' And the woman was healed at that moment" (Matt. 9:22).
- "I will do whatever you ask in my name, so that the Father may be glorified in the Son" (John 14:13).
- "You may ask me for anything in my name, and I will do it" (John 14:14).
- "I have told you these things, so that in me you may have peace. In this world you will have trouble. But take heart! I have overcome the world" (John 16:33).
- "My God will meet all your needs according to the riches of his glory in Christ Jesus" (Phil. 4:19).
- "Keep your lives free from the love of money and be content with what you have, because God has said, 'Never will I leave you; never will I forsake you'" (Heb. 13:5).

I had ample promises from God that healing was within the scope of my warranty. Of course, God had the prerogative to decide when my healing would occur—either in life or in heaven—but one way or another, my healing was guaranteed. This assured me that God was with me and I did not have to be lonely.

DEFEATING THE NO OF LONELINESS

Mr. Blind Man also had his life history to combat the no of being alone. He was well-known as someone who sat and begged on a daily basis (see John 9:8). He may not have had people to bring goods to his house or escort him through the streets of his town, but he was not entirely without support. He would not have continued to go out and beg every day unless there were those who provided support. That means that although he may have been momentarily by himself, he was not alone.

That was the basis of his believing that going outside his house was a wiser decision than remaining in. The first part of his journey from inside to outside may have been a solo flight, but he had enough experience to be guided by past successes rather than his current status.

Granted, Mr. Blind Man was not diagnosed with a life-threatening disease, as I was. Also, he had been afflicted with blindness for quite a long time. One could conclude that since he had been blind all his life, he should have adjusted to the condition and gotten accustomed to dealing with it alone. But being alone affects everyone differently.

Some people who have faced challenges alone for a long time wake up one morning and snap. They have just had enough. It may have appeared to others that all was well with those people, but that was simply because no one could see the loneliness inside.

What about you, my friend? Are you bottling up your loneliness? Do you feel it rising up and threatening to burst out, even onto those you love? That's normal, but it doesn't have to be this way. Others can come alongside you and help you bear this burden.

Mr. Blind Man taught me to lean heavily on the memories that reminded me there would always be some person—a family member, a coworker, a friend, or a neighbor—who would be company for me. Just as people had given Mr. Blind Man charity gifts all his life, I too would be supported by others. I was alone, but I did not have to become lonely.

As you may have guessed, the first person I told about my cancer was my wife. I was actually tempted not to tell her, at least not right away. I didn't want her to be worried. I wanted to shield her from the impact and the fears that might come. But I knew that if I tried to deal with this challenge alone, I would become lonely. If I became lonely, I might even mistreat her, and that would hurt our relationship. As soon as I told her I had cancer, the no of loneliness was immediately defeated in me.

I extended that victory in my closest circles. The more I shared my challenge with my sons, my church leaders, and my congregation, the more support I received and the more I realized I was not alone. So many people shared their stories about their bouts with cancer. And most importantly, so many people promised to pray for me, a blessed task they would not have been able to undertake had I kept my issue private and tried to cope alone.

SOLITUDE IS REDEMPTIVE

There is a distinct difference between loneliness and solitude.

Loneliness is a feeling of abandonment, detachment, and isolation that undermines one's joy and optimism. Loneliness provokes feelings of unworthiness and being unwanted. Loneliness can attack the spiritual infrastructure of the most successful religious leader and cause destruction similar to the impact termites have on a building. For a long time, the termites operate underground and the external structure of the building looks beautiful. Then, all of a sudden, the termite-ridden structure collapses, revealing the damage.

Loneliness functions like that. No one is exempt. Elijah experienced this loneliness while hiding in a cave from Jezebel's wrath (see 1 Kings 19).

Solitude, on the other hand, is time alone. Solitude can have great redemptive value. My wife spent years wondering why it takes me so long to take showers. If we both need to get ready, she rushes into the shower before I can get there, because she knows she will be late if she waits for me. Technically, I am in the shower alone. But instead of my aloneness turning into loneliness, it becomes solitude. Not only does the shower cleanse my body; it also provides time for thinking, meditating, and praying. Solitude is when being alone has a redemptive purpose. Solitude can contribute to our well-being.

One of my heroes is Viktor Frankl, a Jewish victim of Nazi oppression who wrote about how he turned his years in concentration camps into a time of personal renewal. Chuck Colson, a man convicted in the infamous Watergate scandal of the 1970s, turned his prison cell into a place of solitude and allowed God to give him a new mission for his life.

Both of these men could have become overwhelmed by their aloneness, but instead, they said no to loneliness and yes to solitude—they redefined their reality into something that served their needs.

I don't like the expression "Everything happens for a reason." That can be an uninspiring statement if you never find out what the reason is. Perhaps a better thing to say might be "Everything that happens is an opportunity." When the no of being alone happens, we can redefine it as a yes of solitude. Then our alone time can be a blessed space for reflection, contemplation, and prayer.

I have always been impressed and challenged by the monastic movements, especially those that involve a simple life focused on prayer. I love the value that monasticism places on spending time alone with God, seeing prayer as a lifestyle and not merely an event. From the early fourth century up to the current moment, monks and others committed to the monastic lifestyle are the ultimate role models for inviting the no of loneliness into their lives and turning it into a powerful experience of maintaining intimacy with God.

The monastic model of solitude represents an institutional approach to proactively arresting loneliness and converting it into solitude. Not many of us will become monks, but all of us can learn how to defy the threat of being alone and bypass loneliness to achieve a state of solitude.

Mr. Blind Man taught me all this. Had he been a lonely man, his entire day would have been different. But because he said no to loneliness, he was able to muster the strength to leave his house and have an encounter with Jesus that changed his life forever.

TURNING YOUR NO INTO A YES

1. What is your response to aloneness? Do you avoid being alone? Do you seek out alone times? Does aloneness move quickly to loneliness for you? Do you often feel alone even in a crowd?

2. What techniques have you found to be most helpful in preventing your aloneness from

becoming loneliness? If you do become lonely, what things help you come out of that state?

3. If you enjoy solitude, what is it you like about it? If it's been a struggle for you to find value in solitude, what's a new way you could approach it that might feel comfortable for you?

3

THE NO OF BEING JUDGED

When I was in sixth grade, my teacher told me that *if* I ever did manage to graduate from high school, I would end up in jail.

Her words cut to the core of my soul. I was twelve years old—old enough to understand that my teacher had concluded I had no meaningful future beyond my high school years. It was clear to me that my family's race, our income, and my behavioral flaws had combined to cause my teacher to believe there was a huge no awaiting me. She had prejudged me in a way that could have caused me to give up on my future.

I didn't believe her, though.

There had been too many people in my life who had taught me to believe in myself, my gifts, and the God who had made me. I had loving parents and praying grandmothers and supportive church members. That was the very same year I started my career in public speaking. I was drafted to give the welcome address at a program at our church. In the same year that she tried to give me a no, I was given the yes that would lead to me becoming a public speaker for a living.

My saying yes when my teacher said no meant that I had to be determined to prove her wrong. Rather than being intimidated or demoralized by her words, I allowed them to motivate me for the rest of my life. Every time I gave extra effort to a project, every time I spent extra time studying for a test, even when I was given positions that I had no previous experience with handling, I used my teacher's low opinion as my fuel.

When I speak to young people, I often urge them to make a list of the people who doubt their future success and keep that list handy. Then I advise them to do what I did after I became New Jersey secretary of state. I looked up that teacher's address and sent her one of my business cards. I told her that she had been wrong about my future. You may want to make a list of your "no-sayers" and do something similar. It just felt so good!

At the tender age of twelve, I found myself having to say yes to the no of being judged by my teacher. The no of being judged … it can hurt so deeply. It can knock us down so hard that we can't get up. We can start to wonder whether it might be better not to try than to risk getting slammed down that hard again.

Mr. Blind Man had the same challenge in John 9.

THE NO-SAYERS CAN'T STOP YOU

When my teacher looked at me, she saw someone who had little value. She didn't see a whole person with great worth and potential.

My guess is that most people saw Mr. Blind Man in the same way. He was a beggar—and a disabled beggar, at that. He wasn't a regular person. He was one of the inevitables of a large city, perhaps, but not someone with worth and potential. If anything, he might be good as an object lesson, someone to be talked about as if he weren't actually sitting there listening.

That's how the disciples treated him when they asked Jesus about him. They didn't see a valuable human being, a fellow Jew, who happened to be born blind—just as my teacher didn't see a student who happened to be black. The disciples saw a blind man whose condition was important but whose person-hood and potential were not—just as my teacher saw skin color and social status as being more important than my personhood and potential. The disciples, like my teacher, saw the man's con-dition as a kind of moral failure.

Their question to Jesus gives this away. "Who sinned?" they asked (John 9:2). They wanted to know whose sin it was—Mr. Blind Man's or his parents'—that God had punished by causing him to be born blind. Someone had sinned; they knew that without even thinking about it. The only question was who had done the sinning.

It's an insulting question right from the start. And they didn't even have the decency to wait until the man was out of earshot before asking it. He was blind not deaf! But you don't owe respect to someone who isn't fully human, apparently.

Their first question could have been "Jesus, since You have the power, won't You please heal this man of his blindness so he can be released into his potential?" By this time they were familiar with Jesus' compassion. He had displayed it when He fed the multitudes (see ch. 6). They certainly knew He had the power necessary to heal this man. He'd displayed that power when He healed the man by the pool (see ch. 5). If they'd not given Mr. Blind Man the no of judgment, they might've expressed concern for his hardship.

However, the disciples were more concerned about Mr. Blind Man's spiritual rap sheet than his future possibilities. They had objectified Mr. Blind Man to the extent that his blindness dominated their view of him. He was nothing to them but his disability, and they had questions about the topic of disabilities.

One of the most painful experiences in life is to be prejudged by other people. Prejudice and discrimination are nothing but prejudging someone. Unfortunately every society throughout history has subjected certain people to this dehumanizing and demoralizing treatment. The genesis of the say yes movement among my grandmother's church members stemmed from the no of prejudicial treatment blacks received from the larger society in the nineteenth and twentieth centuries. This maltreatment was based on race.

American society, influenced by incorrect biblical interpretation, had concluded that enslaved Africans and their descendants had been permanently assigned a status of servitude because of the so-called curse of Ham:

> Noah, a man of the soil, proceeded to plant a vineyard. When he drank some of its wine, he became drunk and lay uncovered inside his tent. Ham, the father of Canaan, saw his father naked and told his two brothers outside. But Shem and Japheth took a garment and laid it across their shoulders; then they walked in backward and covered their father's naked body. Their faces were turned the other way so that they would not see their father naked.
>
> When Noah awoke from his wine and found out what his youngest son had done to him, he said, "Cursed be Canaan! The lowest of slaves will he be to his brothers." (Gen. 9:20–25)

The mishandlers of God's words failed to recognize a few essential things about this "curse." First, the curse was not against Ham but against his son Canaan. It was fulfilled when the descendants of Canaan became servants to the descendants of Shem in the Land of Promise (see Josh. 17:12–13).

It is also important to note that the curse was given not by God but by Noah. A proper reading of the Scripture shows us that the descendants of Canaan were not the Africans who would ultimately be enslaved. Most importantly, these believers should've remembered that Christianity inherently opposes racism, prejudice, and injustice (see, for example, Gal. 3:28).

This faulty interpretation functioned as a biblical foundation for the enslavement of Africans (and the system of South African apartheid). But this one passage of Scripture—wrongly understood—has wreaked racial havoc on the entire world. There are still people today, many of them Christians, who believe God cursed black people and that blacks must remain separate from whites because of the so-called curse of Ham.

We must all remain vigilant against shaky interpretations of Scripture, especially when those interpretations benefit us and harm someone else. Sometimes we don't look too closely at an interpretation that helps our cause, even if it hurts other people. Switch the situation around in your mind until you or your children are the ones being hurt by the interpretation, and see whether you still want to stay silent about how it may actually be incorrect.

One need only consider the damage this kind of prejudice has done to understand the pain it creates. And prejudice is not all racial. Humans make decisions about one another all the time based solely on external and superficial factors. These decisions and thoughts are often reinforced by media and advertising that contain both explicit and subliminal messages about beauty, intelligence, fitness, popularity, health, success, and prosperity.

Learned from childhood, benign preferences can grow into lethal prejudices if not disrupted by a redeemed, converted heart that is molded and shaped by Jesus. I may write a book one day to address those who have been harmed by the plague of prejudice.

Mr. Blind Man was such a man.

OTHER PEOPLE'S EXPERIENCES

Many businesses get started by using other people's money (OPM). Generally, the source for this money is either lenders or investors.

Similarly, people can get started on their journey to yes by using OPE: other people's *experiences*. We can use OPE to overcome life's obstacles, gain higher productivity, and have a more effective ministry. OPE can help us construct strategies for success. Just as we can be the recipients of financial loans or investments, we can be the beneficiaries of other people's experiences by borrowing from their stories and the investments they make in us.

The Bible is a marvelous encyclopedia of stories that can inform us as we seek ideas to form our yes responses when life says no. What I like about OPE is that it doesn't cost anything to use. Their stories are there for us to use. In that sense, the Bible gives us interest-free loans. These stories are part of God's investment in our lives.

Mr. Blind Man of John 9 is a perfect example of another's experiences that we can all use for free!

POSSIBILITIES OUTNUMBER PROBLEMS

Whenever I speak about saying yes when life says no, the most frequently asked question is where to begin. That is what we're looking at in this chapter.

Mr. Blind Man taught me that my possibilities always outnumber my problems. This is crucial to remember when you need to say yes though life is saying no.

Notice at the beginning of John 9 that it says Jesus saw a man who had been blind from birth (see v. 1). John didn't mention that Jesus *and His disciples* saw a man who had been blind from birth. I get the distinct impression that initially only Jesus saw Mr. Blind Man, and then the disciples asked their prejudiced question only after they'd followed His gaze and seen Mr. Blind Man themselves.

Jesus is the master at drawing our attention to the things He wants to work on in us. He knows just the right wrench to throw in our gears to make us ask the questions He's wanting to teach us the answers to.

If He had not caused the disciples to notice Mr. Blind Man, they would not have had their bad theology corrected, Mr. Blind Man would not have received his sight, and we would not be learning all these amazing things from the story.

If I had never gotten prostate cancer, I might never have been drawn back to this story with such urgency, and God might never have taught me these life-changing lessons.

As a result of my intensive study of John 9, I developed a long list of strategies. They are things I saw Mr. Blind Man doing. And they are things you and I can apply to our own lives. These strategies have proved useful in my life, my ministry, my government service, my organizational affiliations, and my corporate positions.

Here's a sampling of those strategies:

- I have to look beyond the reality of my current circumstances.
- I have to take inventory of what I have and not be overwhelmed by what I don't have.
- I have to expect new possibilities despite the reality of existing problems. Because possibilities outnumber problems.
- I must not wait for others to notice or accept me before saying yes to any of life's nos.

I learned all this from only the opening verses of John 9!

TOO BUSY TO NOTICE

So as Jesus "went along, he saw a man blind from birth" (v. 1). As an itinerant Jewish teacher, it was normal for Him to move about with a band of students. When people walk together in a small group and one person's attention is drawn to something, it's not unreasonable that at least part of the group would look in the same direction—especially if that person is the leader.

It's natural, then, that the disciples asked about what Jesus was looking at. But I wonder whether Jesus had been hoping that they would notice Mr. Blind Man on their own, without Him having to draw their attention. Apparently, they had not. It's sad when people are so busy doing whatever they do that they miss seeing another human.

It happens to the best of us. I know it happened to me.

I was in Washington, DC, to attend a meeting. I arrived so early that I had time to grab lunch at a nearby restaurant. A young woman who worked for the organization I was visiting offered to show me to the restaurant. On our way, she shared with me that she was an atheist.

That was all I needed to hear. I determined to witness to her and lead her to Christ by the time we reached the restaurant. After all, that is what I do. I had preached to and led thousands of people to accept Jesus as their Savior. Indeed, I believed this one young atheist should be easy to convince that Jesus is Lord and she should receive His love.

While I was thinking about the words I would use to share Christ with her, I had not realized that she was no longer walking next to me toward the restaurant. I turned to see where she had gone. I finally spotted her a half block up the street, talking to a man sitting on the road. I was alarmed because this fellow begging on the street was a black man and this young woman was white. The dangerous possibilities of what was happening raced through my mind. I immediately went into rescue mode and sprinted up the street to help this young maiden.

When I reached the homeless man and the atheist woman, I heard her say, "Good-bye, Richard."

What? She knew his name? Yes, she did. As we walked away, she told me that he sits there every day begging for money and that she talks with him. She considered him her friend. I had never even seen the man! I was so busy preparing to tell this young atheist about the love of Jesus that my clergy self never even saw the man sitting on the sidewalk.

This atheist taught me that I should never be too busy to notice someone despite that person's station in life. I had done what I believe those disciples did. Jesus saw Mr. Blind Man, but His disciples didn't.

DON'T WAIT TO BE SEEN

To be unnoticed can have a negative impact on people's self-esteem. To be ignored can cause people to wonder whether something is wrong with them. While it is rarely fatal, if life has said no to people a sufficient number of times, just being ignored may push them over the edge and cause them to do something terrible. We have seen too many instances of alienated people responding to their pain with acts that injure other people.

So as I watch Mr. Blind Man stand by and say nothing as these men walk past him, I admire him greatly. He could have had an outburst of some kind and demanded the attention and recognition of the disciples. But John described Mr. Blind Man as saying nothing. That becomes even more profound when he also resists the temptation to respond personally to the insulting question asked about him.

You will never say yes to life's nos if you insist that other people notice and accept you. Don't get me wrong—it's wonderful to have friends and associates. It's a great feeling when people send birthday cards and anniversary acknowledgments. It was so encouraging to hear from people who were praying for me as I approached my surgery. But Mr. Blind Man taught me that I could not wait for others to recognize me before I got started with my yes lifestyle.

Although I may enjoy the recognition of others, it's dangerous to see it as a prerequisite to feel that I can make it to my destination. It is likely that Mr. Blind Man sensed he was in the presence of a group. That suspicion was confirmed when at least one of the disciples acknowledged his existence by asking who sinned.

This was already the fourth no Mr. Blind Man had to deal with in this little episode. The first was his blindness. The next was that he was alone on this particular day. The third was being ignored by the guys with Jesus and being noticed only by Jesus. This fourth was being exposed to the judgmental question raised by one or more of Jesus' disciples.

"Who sinned, this man or his parents, that he was born blind?" (v. 2). This question was interesting to them as a theological exercise. Whatever the answer might be to the doctrinal query, it was certainly not going to be helpful to Mr. Blind Man. Here was a man whose livelihood came from begging, yet these passersby were more concerned about his moral character and lineage than his immediate needs. He had become an object lesson.

At the very least, they could have given him a contribution before turning to the question of his moral identity. Then they could've asked him about it instead of talking over him. Or they could have chosen to share with the man the great news about Jesus and who He was. What a concept, huh?

Not one of the disciples decided to do any of those things. They didn't address him at all. They decided to talk about the man instead of talking to him. Mr. Blind Man was standing right there—they could have easily asked him what they wanted to know about him. But they did not care about my friend Mr. Blind Man. They were interested in his sins, and they ignored him as a human.

But Mr. Blind Man was not bothered by this at all. He remained steadfast, and his day ended just fine. Better than fine, in fact.

VALUE THE RIGHT KIND OF ACKNOWLEDGMENT

The fact that the disciples didn't ask Jesus about Mr. Blind Man until Jesus noticed him is quite interesting. Some people notice us only after someone they admire pays attention to us or when we become perceived as competition.

After I was featured in *Almighty Debt*, a ninety-minute documentary on CNN with Soledad O'Brien, I started getting phone calls from people I knew didn't like me. I was the same person with the same goals and ideologies I'd had before the documentary. But suddenly they saw me in a new light, and a new respect miraculously dawned in their minds. Now I could help them, or now I was "somebody," or now I was important, so they found a way to get past their dislike and give me a friendly phone call.

The disciples couldn't be bothered to acknowledge Mr. Blind Man until Jesus paid attention to him. But even then, they were more concerned about asking Jesus why Mr. Blind Man was born without sight than paying attention to his presence and his immediate need. They didn't even ask Jesus whether they could give him a donation. They cared more about the man's sins than they cared about his needs. He still wasn't a real person to them, but his existence might be a tool to get some of their questions answered.

Although Mr. Blind Man may have heard the disciples talking about him—talking insultingly about him—he did not say a word. He was calm and quiet.

Here is another valuable lesson we can learn from him: you don't always have to react when people judge you, even if they do so within your hearing. Remain calm and quiet. You never know whether responding to people's negativity toward you might cause you to miss your blessing.

Mr. Blind Man could have reacted to the disciples and gotten into an argument with them about his background. He could've made a scene and defended his parents and called insults down on these insensitive men. But he'd probably learned the hard way that mouthing off to potential donors was a good way to miss out on donations. Jesus could have moved on to heal someone else if Mr. Blind Man had argued with the disciples.

Here is Jesus' response to the disciples' question: "Neither this man nor his parents sinned … but this happened so that the works of God might be displayed in him. As long as it is day, we must do the works of him who sent me. Night is coming, when no one can work. While I am in the world, I am the light of the world" (vv. 3–5).

To me, Jesus was implying that if they really cared about Mr. Blind Man and weren't merely gossiping, they would have inquired how they could help him rather than wonder why he was born blind.

I imagine it must've been so satisfying for Mr. Blind Man to hear someone defend his character like this. I imagine he was very glad he had managed to hold his tongue.

If you answer every fool, if you argue with every hater, if you are distracted by every question or comment, you will surely miss a significant blessing. There will always be someone in your life trying to distract you with things that don't matter. This distraction can even emanate from people we consider our friends.

We have to be careful with whom we associate, because many of our friends and acquaintances may not have our best interests at heart. You can identify such individuals when, in your time of need, they focus more on probing into how you ended up in that situation than determining how they can help you out of it. Or they just disappear from your life entirely.

There are people in every community who are expert analysts of other people's situations. They have a ready explanation for everything. They can explain why so many people are incarcerated, but they will never visit or interact with somebody in jail. They can tell why the foster care system is bursting at the seams, but they will never adopt or foster a child. They can explain why so many people are in debt, but they do nothing to help somebody get out of debt. They can offer penetrating sociological and psychological analysis, but they don't lift a finger to help. Some people have what Dr. Martin Luther King Jr. would call "paralysis of analysis."[1]

SIN AND SICKNESS

In Jesus' day and culture, the common belief was that every instance of sickness came from sin. Not only sickness but misfortune of all kinds were thought to be caused by sin.

When calamity fell on Job, his friends' core assumption was that Job had sinned to bring the disaster on himself. If only he would confess and repent, God might ease up (see 8:5–6; 22:21–30). Job fought that false theology (see 27:1–6; 31:1–40), yet it seemed to still be the prevailing belief in Jewish culture many centuries later.

In a sense, of course, it is true. All illness does exist because of the sin of Adam and Eve. Further, Scripture tells us that particular sins inflict pain on us and have consequences that can even be passed along to our children and their children (see Ex. 34:7). From one point of view, all death, illness, and catastrophe *does* stem from sin, that first sin in Eden. But what isn't true is that every bad thing that happens to you is God's punishment for your sin.

That's why Jesus tackled that false doctrine here and in other places, such as when He asked whether the people who were killed when the tower of Siloam fell on them were worse sinners than anyone else (see Luke 13:4–5).

The disciples thought this man's blindness was an illustration of someone's sin. But Jesus answered that his blindness was to be an illustration of God's power.

Mr. Blind Man's no had been put there on purpose so God could work a glorious yes.

Consider that your no also may have been placed there on purpose by God so He can turn it into a magnificent yes.

This story encourages us to understand God as allowing specific occurrences to happen to people without regard to their behaviors or choices. Further, Jesus wanted His disciples to stop analyzing Mr. Blind Man's problem and get involved in the solution instead.

Jesus and the disciples did not share the same perspective on what they saw before them. The disciples turned to Jesus and inquired about why Mr. Blind Man lost his sight, while Jesus focused on how Mr. Blind Man would *gain* his sight.

The good news about my teacher's prejudgment is that it ended up not mattering. Not only did I finish high school; I was also senior class president, and I gave the speech at my graduation ceremony. I have since earned bachelor's, master's, and doctorate degrees, and I have had a great professional and ministerial career.

The good news about Mr. Blind Man is that he did not allow the assumptions of the disciples to stop him from taking advantage of his opportunity to receive his sight from Jesus.

In order for us to begin to say yes to life's nos, we must imitate Mr. Blind Man's resilience and choose to push forward even though forces and people around us may be trying to hold us down.

TURNING YOUR NO INTO A YES

1. What is the most discouraging, disempowering thing anyone has ever said to you? Did it cause you to give up on a dream? In what ways did it cause you to change course or shift your definition of yourself? In what ways might it still be affecting you today—negatively or positively?

2. Think about a time when you had to bite your tongue while someone said something insensitive or hurtful about you or someone you cared about. How were you able to hold your silence? Did staying quiet result in a blessing? Think about a time when you didn't hold your tongue. Did that result in a blessing?

3. How do you respond to the idea that prejudice is a way to dehumanize someone else? Do you agree? The disciples didn't consider Mr. Blind Man worthy of the respect they would give a full person. Who has treated you as less than a full person? Think about a time when you caught yourself considering someone not your equal and not worthy of respect. What are the dangers of beginning to dehumanize another person?

4

THE NO OF NEGATIVE PEOPLE

Whom do you hang around with? Who is your squad? Unless you're very intentional about broadening your circle, the people you keep closest will be the ones who reflect who you are and who you are going to be. In a sense, you are the average of the five people you hold as your closest friends.

Do the people you spend time with pull you closer to Jesus or further away?

The Christian faith is often described as a walk. Imagine that you lived in New Testament times and you had the chance to join either a group that was walking close to Jesus or another group that was walking away from Him. The group you choose—in Bible times or today—will either help you stay close to the Lord or tend to pull you away from Him.

Mr. Blind Man was exposed to negativity and condescension from the disciples. He didn't have to sit there and take that. He could've gotten up and made his way home or to some other part of the city. But despite their prejudice and insensitivity, he decided to stay close enough to Jesus to receive what he needed.

Have you ever encountered such negativity that you walked away from a blessing? Has someone's discouragement ever caused you to back off from advocating for something you thought was important? What could be more of a no than negativity? But Mr. Blind Man shows us that we don't have to miss out on a massive blessing just because negative people stand in the way.

The people in Jesus' inner circle, the disciples, were concerned only about the past sins of Mr. Blind Man and his parents. But he was not deterred by their criticism, and he determined to stay close to Jesus.

When we are striving to be the person we were made to be, we should understand the value of staying close to Jesus. Negative people sometimes fill the church and can make us feel as if we should just back away from Jesus. But the blessing we need is found only when we stay close to Jesus.

CHOOSE YOUR FRIENDS WISELY

You cannot be too careful about whom you choose to learn from. Some people will teach you how to get to your yes, but there will always be others who want you to settle for a no. I have learned to tell the difference between positive and negative role models. You must be able to do this too, or you will confuse fleeting fame with consistent greatness.

When I was a very young man, I spent a lot of time studying famous people. I wanted to be like them, and I at first counted myself blessed that I ended up working right next to some of those very people.

It is an interesting thing to work next to men and women who have been your heroes and heroines from a distance. What I discovered about famous people is that sometimes they are a greater blessing to you from a distance.

Because I have had the fortune of working closely with so many people who have high public recognition, I have learned—in more ways than I am willing to disclose—that it is better not to know them personally. The closer I got to some famous people, the more disappointed I became.

Some people can help you say yes when life says no. Some cannot. You must be very careful and selective about whom you get close to.

Most of us are not still close to the people we were close to twenty years ago. Some of us cannot remember the names of half the people we were close to even just ten years ago. And many of us *are* close to people whose names we would like to forget.

Since you're reading this book, I'm going to assume that you are trying to get beyond some no in your life and get to some yes. Maybe you're trying to be a better parent, a better employee, a better Christian, a better woman or man, a better servant, or a better citizen. Maybe you're attempting to improve your life financially, intellectually, emotionally, or spiritually. Whatever yes you're pursuing, the chances are good that you cannot do it all by yourself.

This thought creates a two-sided problem for me. On one hand, I have to be super selective about whom I am close to. Yet, on the other, I cannot get to my yes all by myself.

Let's bring it back to Mr. Blind Man as an example. Here was a man who had to be extra careful about whom he got close to. He had no way of reading facial expressions or body language, of course. If he trusted the wrong people, they could rip him off—steal from him—and he wouldn't know it. Even worse, they could negatively affect his emotional state. Mr. Blind Man must have already been frustrated, having been marginalized and forced to beg for a living. One small mistake of allying with the wrong person could make a bad situation worse.

Think about the people you spend most of your time with. I'm mainly thinking about peers, but certain family members may need to be included. Do you trust them? Have you chosen your friends wisely?

Mr. Blind Man did not know Jesus at all. At this point in the story, even if he somehow knew Jesus' name, he likely had no idea who Jesus was, how He had been born, who had baptized Him, or what any of the miracles were that Jesus had done. In fact, in John 9:11, when asked how he had received his sight, Mr. Blind Man said it was "the man they call Jesus."

He had not known a single detail about Jesus except for the fact that He gave him his sight.

Yet somehow, though he knew next to nothing about Jesus, Mr. Blind Man was still able to comprehend that Jesus was exactly the person he needed to draw close to. He sensed that Jesus was someone he could trust to get him beyond all the nos that confronted him. So he stayed close to Jesus.

WHY AND HOW TO STAY CLOSE TO JESUS

Why did he hang around? I imagine Mr. Blind Man, after overhearing the disciples' question, would have strained to hear whether Jesus would give an answer rooted in Greek reincarnation philosophy—that penalties for certain sins in life showed up in a physical form in the next life. Or whether maybe Jesus would quote the Jewish belief system of prenatal sin—that a person could sin while still only a fetus in the womb and be born with an infirmity as a result.

I imagine that Mr. Blind Man, having grown up hearing such explanations for his infirmity, was listening to find out which one Jesus would use. But through it all he remained right there and waited. If it had been me, I would've reacted vociferously and left the vicinity.

At this point in my research of John 9, I was determined to find out why Mr. Blind Man stayed close to Jesus. I concluded that if staying close to Jesus caused this blind man to finish his day seeing, then Jesus could also do in my life something like what He'd done in Mr. Blind Man's life … if I only stayed close to Him.

How do you stay close to Jesus? The most obvious answer is that you stay in a running conversation with Him in prayer. Prayer, Scripture reading, meditation, worship, and journaling are great ways to keep your heart near His. Going to church *can* be another way, and I hope it usually is for you, but when we start adding other humans into the formula, sometimes there can be challenges. Church attendance is often a way to stay close to Jesus, but I want to say that the two are not necessarily synonymous.

So that's the how of staying close to Jesus. Now let's look at the why.

I discovered a major reason Mr. Blind Man stayed where he was—close to Jesus—when he had every right to walk away.

Jesus never judged him. Here were the representatives of the church, as it were, probing into the moral cause of his infirmity. They were ready to explain it away as the result of the sins of his parents or him. They looked down their noses at him in judgment. But Jesus stopped them in their tracks and said that the cause wasn't sin at all.

Have you ever been in a situation where people think they know things about you? A position where they think they have found your weakness and will tell your most intimate secrets to anyone who will listen, especially when that information is inaccurate?

The tragedy is that we tend to internalize the negative things people say about us. Those chickens have a habit of settling in to roost. If you let people call you dumb long enough, you start to see dumb when you look in the mirror. If you listen to people telling you how lazy you are often enough, you end up staying in bed until noon every day. If you hear people calling you ugly, you come to believe you are ugly and you begin to buy all kinds of beauty products. Our belief determines our behavior.

All the "isms" we hate in our culture—racism, sexism, ageism, etc.—are just ways for one group to look down on another group to feel superior. On the other side of it, when people are put down or prejudged enough, they tend to develop an inferiority complex, believing what's said about them.

Yet Mr. Blind Man did not succumb! He stood his ground. He stayed where he was, despite the negative conjecture and gossip occurring right in front of him. Because he realized that Jesus saw him as a person beloved by God and deserving of respect. Jesus dismissed sin as the explanation for his blindness and instead saw him as a man who just happened to be blind.

If he had vented his hurt and anger and fled from the scene, he never would've received the blessing of that affirmation. Or the greater blessing that was to come.

WHEN CHRISTIANS OFFEND YOU

People tend to abandon their faith just because other believers do not treat them well. Many have stopped going to church simply because the pastor or a member said something that, to them, seemed offensive or "shady."

This happens even with ministers of the gospel, I'm ashamed to say. If the people in their church—the members and deacons and trustees and staff and volunteers—don't treat the pastor as a pastor "should" be treated, that pastor may move on to another church or even to another religion entirely.

I learned something from Mr. Blind Man in this Scripture: you can't let other people's negativity be the no that keeps you from God's yes. It isn't Jesus doing that to you—it's the flawed people around Him. So what if the people around Jesus do not treat me nicely? Why should that stop me from staying close to Jesus Himself?

How is it with you? Have you let some followers of Jesus turn you away from following Him? Have you seen that happen in the lives of others? Isn't that a shame? I can't tell you how many ex-church members have told me that they dropped out of church because of something someone said. I think it's very sad, but it also makes me a little angry. Angry at the person who said the dumb thing, obviously. But angry also that the people who let someone come between them and Jesus.

Are we really going to quit something good when someone is unkind to us? Some members of a club or organization may not treat you well, but wouldn't you stay involved if you gained a lot from being part of the organization? The manager of a retail store may not take the time to greet you each time you frequent the business, but the store has the best-quality products and prices, so won't you keep going back? These kinds of situations happen all around us, but we should never let them make us give up on something good.

Are you really going to let someone's irresponsible comment keep you away from the Savior of the world? Just because someone you thought was close to God says or does something to offend you, will that be the thing that causes you to stop reading your Bible or going to church—or believing in the power of God? Don't let that person's no keep you from God's yes. Go to another church. Join a new Bible study class. Enroll in a different theological seminary.

Do whatever is necessary to stay close to Jesus, no matter what!

Mr. Blind Man must have thought, *These disciples are in my business. But guess what? I'm staying right here on my street corner, close to this man they call Jesus. He speaks up in my defense, and who knows what else He can do for me?* Who knew, indeed!

Mr. Blind Man's response was based not on the actions or words of the people around Jesus but on the character of Jesus Himself. It was based on the fact that he was able to trust Jesus in that brief encounter where Jesus defended him and said, "While I am in the world, I am the light of the world" (John 9:5).

LIGHT IN THE DARKNESS

Sometimes we overlook the severity of Mr. Blind Man's disability. Unlike those who start their lives with sight but then lose their vision along the way, this man had never seen the light of day. He had been blind when he emerged from his mother's womb. He had been in absolute darkness throughout his child-hood and his entire adult life up to that moment.

Whatever development his brain would've undergone if his eyes had been working had simply never happened. Or perhaps there was damage to his brain that caused the blindness. His blindness was profound and complete.

Anyone who has experienced total darkness, a pitch-black environment, will agree that if there is one thing a person in darkness needs, it is light. Sunlight, candlelight, torchlight, moonlight—anything would do!

A man in total darkness really, really hears it when a fellow says, "I am the light." Think about that. When Mr. Blind Man heard Jesus say that, he was immediately drawn to Him like a moth to a flame. He had never met anyone who was bold enough and self-confident enough to say that he or she was *everything* he needed—the solution to his every problem.

Try making a list of all the people in your life who claimed to have everything you needed and who then delivered on their prom-ise. I'm guessing your list won't have any names. Not one! No one is capable of meeting your every need. Love songs aside, no human is capable of looking you in the face and saying with certainty that he or she will always provide you with whatever you need.

We need a guide. We need a light in the darkness.

Your doctor doesn't have everything you need, even just for your health. If you went to your cardiologist with pain in your feet, he would have to refer you to another doctor. Your spouse doesn't have everything you need. Your children definitely can't give you everything you need—and you can't guarantee you can always give them everything they need. No politician can give you everything you need, and no slick marketer online can give you everything you need.

Yet we need *someone* to give us what we lack. We can't do it alone, but no one can give us all we need.

We admit that we cannot get past the no in our lives all on our own. We cannot read ourselves there, jog our way there, eat our way there, self-medicate our way there, or even learn to get there. We need a role model we can emulate, a dependable someone who will pick us up when we stumble, encourage us when we want to give up, inspire us when we lose hope, and cheer for us when we achieve.

Praise God—we have such a one!

The only person who has ever claimed to have everything you need—and proved the claim true—is Jesus! He said, "Seek first his kingdom and his righteousness, and all these things will be given to you as well" (Matt. 6:33).

Take it from me: if you have been wondering whether Jesus is Jesus—whether Jesus is really God and whether He can change you—join a Bible-believing church and stick around (stay close to Jesus) to experience His life-changing power for yourself. He is the light in the darkness.

In many ways, my wife has been all I ever needed. I tell her this often. However, when I am in an airplane thirty thousand feet in the air and we run into severe turbulence and I see the flight attendant fastening his or her seat belt, my wife is not everything I need. Wonderful as she is, she can't help me in a situation like that.

Similarly, when I went into surgery to remove cancer from my body and was given a dose of anesthesia and then asked to count backward from ten to one, by the time I got to seven, I was in oblivion and my wife couldn't help me. I needed somebody more powerful than my wife. At moments like that, I need someone who can command the storm to be still and the wind to be quiet (see Mark 4:39). I need someone who can put the ocean to sleep and lay flat the great mountains (see Isa. 45:2).

No mayor, governor, teacher, preacher, deacon, or trustee can do that. The pope can't do that, nor can the most seasoned prophet or healer. You can attend all the conferences and workshops you want, you can listen to all the sermons you wish, you can read all the motivational books you can collect, and you won't have that kind of power. You can practice yoga or tai chi, you can light candles and chant, and you can pay therapists and consultants until the cows come home. But if you want to say yes to life's next opportunities, especially after you've done all you can do, you'd better stay close to Jesus.

TIPS FOR STAYING CLOSE TO JESUS

Here is how I stay close to Him and how you can too:

- Have frequent conversations with Jesus (prayer).
- Spend a good amount of time reading the Scriptures and books about Jesus.
- Stay close to people who are trying to stay close to Jesus.
- Participate in worship that keeps the focus on Jesus.

I know famous people. I have been in the Oval Office at the White House. I call celebrities my friends. I have friends in high places who can make a lot of things happen for me. I have been on private jets and luxury yachts. But not one of them was crucified on a cross and raised from the dead for me. Not one of them is the Son of God.

There are some things I can get only from Jesus.

I can have 24-7 access only to Jesus. I can have a flawless role model only in Jesus. I have an uncompromised standard for integrity only in Jesus. I get flawless ethical advice only from Jesus. I get the greatest example of servant leadership only in Jesus. I receive the clearest understanding of God only from Jesus. I possess the guarantee of life after death only through my belief in and relationship with Jesus.

We tend to focus solely on our goals. We can become systematic and methodical in our dealings. We can be so complacent with our status quo that we cease to grow. We can feel we have arrived …

Right up until the moment when the next big tragedy occurs. Or the next hurricane hits our coastlines. Or the devastating diagnosis comes.

Any hurdle we have to jump can make us completely forget who is in charge. Obstacles can make us lose sight of who placed us in the position we are in and who is the only person who can get us out of it, if it is His will.

THE NO WON'T WIPE YOU OUT

True peace and security can be found only in Jesus. To travel the rocky path of no, we need to remind ourselves to always believe that Jesus is alpha and omega—our beginning, our today, and, yes, our end. He remains with us through the turbulence and storms. Whether we are down or up, sick or healthy, we have His steady hand bearing us over the tides.

Before his encounter with Jesus, all Mr. Blind Man knew was this difficult life. He understood begging to make a living, being scorned, getting rejected and stigmatized. He had heard stories made up about him and about his parents. There were days he went to bed hungry because he'd received no alms, and there were days he'd been scorched by the sun or drenched by the rain. Though most days he received enough donations to get by, no one had been able to offer him what he truly needed ... until Jesus saw him on the street that fateful day.

Did you know that Islam requires all Muslims to pray five times a day and give alms to the poor? Muslims must meet specific religious requirements, including ritual ablution and special handling of the Qur'an. I like the structural nature of the five pillars of Islam and how Muslims save money to fulfill a lifelong ambition to go on the hajj, a pilgrimage to Mecca.

The truth is, there are some things Christians could learn from our Muslim friends to help us grow and become less self-centered.

But here's the difference. I may admire Islam, but I cannot get close to Muhammad. Why? Because he is dead. There is an actual tomb at the Prophet's Mosque in the city of Medina in Saudi Arabia, where his remains were laid to rest. No matter how devout, a Muslim can never get close to Muhammad.

Our Lord Jesus died on a Friday afternoon, and He too was laid to rest in a tomb. But on Sunday morning the angel of the Lord rolled away the stone from the entrance of His tomb, and our Jesus rose from the dead (see Matt. 28:1–6). After forty days He ascended into heaven in plain view of several witnesses to take His rightful place at the right hand of the Father (see Acts 1:3–9).

Christians can stay close to Jesus because *He is alive!* "I am the light," Jesus said (John 9:5). But that was not all He said. Jesus also said, "I am the way" (14:6).

The various nos we experience can be enough to make us feel as if life is trying to wipe us out. Getting past no and reaching the next yes in our lives can feel nearly impossible. If you have been down enough times in your life, if you have ever been in pain, if you have ever failed again and again when looking for a job, you know what I mean. If you have lost enough relatives to death or had too many friends turn their backs on you, you know what it feels like to lose your way.

During times of real trouble, you need something more than a social security check to get you through. You need assurance that "God will meet all your needs according to the riches of his glory" in His good time (Phil. 4:19).

When I was a young man, I was confident I could make it on my own. I definitely didn't need Jesus. I could pull myself up by my bootstraps. I also figured there were already so many people in the church that the church didn't need me too. I certainly didn't need to go to church to be a good person. In fact, I found that going to church actually made me meaner because of all the stuck-up churchgoers I would encounter.

Years later, that church hasn't gotten much better. Nor may it ever get better. But now I know that the church and all the people who make up the church are not the pathway to my blessings. I know this because Jesus said, "I am the way."

If you are weighed down with burdens, He gives you peace that passes all understanding (see Phil. 4:7). His Spirit functions the way wind undergirds and uplifts the wings of a bird. The Spirit of God is the presence of Jesus, and He does for us what Jesus did for those He encountered when He was here physically. Just as Jesus helped the weak, the sick, the distressed, and the spiritually possessed, so His Spirit does for us.

Because we are human, we tend to be fearful of the unknown. However, God said that while bad stuff will surely come to this world, we don't have to worry about it. "You will have trouble," He said, but we don't have to fear it because He overcame the world (John 16:33).

So while you are running your daily miles on your treadmill or applying *The 7 Habits of Highly Effective People*, while you are mapping out all your new plans or drawing up your monthly budgets, while you are taking courses to update your skills, keep in mind that you cannot leave Jesus in church. Learn to stay close to Jesus.

Because when all else fails, it is Jesus alone who can bring the extraordinary yes into your life.

Someday you will come to appreciate what my grandma meant when she said, "Can't nobody do me like Jesus." It may be bad grammar, but it is undoubtedly sound doctrine.

TURNING YOUR NO INTO A YES

1. Think about a time when someone in the church said something offensive or discouraging to you. How did it affect your view of Jesus and Christianity?

2. Who is a celebrity (or someone you looked up to) who failed you or let you down? People are just people, even the famous ones, and they have their own faults and sins—even those in ministry. What helps you stay close to Jesus even when people don't live up to His standard?

3. What would you say to someone who has gotten offended by a Christian—either in a one-time episode or perhaps with something longer, as with a Christian upbringing—and has left the church?

5

THE NO OF UNCERTAINTY

What else can happen?

I have had to stop asking that question ... because something else can always happen. And often that something else is life saying no.

Sometimes bad will turn to worse before things get better. Uncertainty about the future can be a big no for people.

What could have been worse for Mr. Blind Man? I mean, he had been blind his entire life—what else could happen? Well, on this particular day, he had wandered out of his house all alone, he had been ignored by passersby, he had been treated as an object lesson, and he had been considered guilty of some sin that had caused his blindness.

What else could happen?

How about if someone spit on him?

This man named Jesus spit into some dirt and placed the mud on Mr. Blind Man's eyes (see John 9:6).

Great. Perfect. Just what he wanted.

Still, for some reason—maybe because he was starting to sense that this Jesus was there to give him a blessing—Mr. Blind Man accepted this indignity.

An observer might have considered this an act of masochism. Mr. Blind Man may have appeared as a complete fool to just sit there and let this stranger abuse him like this! Even a blind person has a right to not be humiliated like that.

I wonder whether uncertainty filled Mr. Blind Man's mind. *Was I wrong about this Jesus? Were the earlier words just a setup so I'd drop my guard and let Him come paint me with spit mud so everyone will laugh at me?* Here again, he could've knocked away Jesus' hands and stumbled off into the city.

But he didn't. Despite the uncertainty he felt, by accepting this mud in his eyes, Mr. Blind Man positioned himself for his miracle. Sometimes we must accept uncertainty and unpleasantness to get where we want to go.

UNCERTAINTY DOESN'T HAVE TO SHUT YOU DOWN

Mr. Blind Man has taught me so much about discovering who I am, whom I have the potential to become, and how I respond to the uncertainties of life. And life is full of changes. If you have never experienced something unpredictable in your life, it is only a matter of time before you do. It doesn't matter how wealthy or healthy you are, and it doesn't matter how educated or well-connected you may be—life's uncertainties can catch you off guard. It is these surprises, these reversals, these *uncertainties* that deliver the message of no.

John 9 teaches us not only how to manage uncertainties but also how to get beyond them. Mr. Blind Man taught me that when I have a problem—when life says no—I don't have to shut down until the issue goes away. There are times in life when problems become so many and pressure becomes so intense that it seems to squeeze the very last ounce of enthusiasm out of your being. But uncertainty doesn't have to put your life on pause.

Sometimes the challenges of life are so overwhelming that you don't feel like facing the world another day. You don't feel like getting out of bed or going to work or talking to anyone at all. But sometimes you have to, even though you don't feel like it. You put yourself through the physical motions of the day, but your attitude sends the message that you don't feel like it.

Mr. Blind Man taught me that even a significant lifelong challenge is no reason to shut down. He was uncertain whether his life would ever change for the better, and he had probably learned not to ask "What else can happen?"

Yet, in spite of his blindness, Mr. Blind Man got up that morning and went out to make a living. He was uncertain about his life. He was uncertain whether he would make enough from his begging to buy his daily bread. He was uncertain how people would treat him. But it didn't make him lock his door and stay in bed. The no of uncertainty didn't hold him down.

NOWHERE TO GO BUT UP

Furthermore, Mr. Blind Man taught me not to care too much about what people think of me—even when they think, say, or do their worst.

People can gossip about you even when you are within earshot, but Mr. Blind Man is the exemplar for not reacting to people talking behind your back. Mr. Blind Man taught me that you don't have to win every argument. You don't have to come out on top. You don't have to gain mastery and "conquer" the situation. He taught me that when things get to the very worst, all they can do then is begin to get better. When things hit rock bottom, there is no way to go but up.

What did Mr. Blind Man think when some stranger spit beside him? It's uncertain. He probably had no idea who Jesus was, and we don't get the sense that he had any spiritual insights about Him. Mr. Blind Man was out on the street begging for his daily food as he had done all his life. He had likely heard people talking about him more times than he could recount.

On top of all his other preexisting problems, he had to listen to a man spit.

We can assume that he had heard people spit before. For one thing, his ears were probably very sensitive. He probably heard every last cough, whisper, hiccup, or expectoration anywhere up and down the street.

Also, as a beggar, a seeming nobody, someone of low status and low esteem, he may have even been the victim of people spitting on him. Too often I read about people who prey on homeless and helpless people, harming them just for fun. Mr. Blind Man may have been exposed to such treatment.

So I don't think Mr. Blind Man was overcome with excitement to hear this man spit so close to him. Had I been in his position, I would probably have ducked or tried to get as far away as possible from the sound of that spit, just in case it was aimed at me.

Mr. Blind Man stayed right where he was, in spite of the uncertainty of what the stranger planned to do. He did not walk away when he overheard the disciples talking about him, and he certainly did not walk away when he heard someone spit.

Have you ever stood in the face of abuse or ridicule and refused to run away? Were you able to remain firmly in your rightful place in spite of the threat of even more abuse?

I'm not saying you should always stay where you are in the face of real abuse. Many times the right choice is to get to safety. But there are times when the blessing that may come can lead us to consider enduring it for a time.

DON'T DODGE YOUR BLESSING

Maybe no one has ever literally spit on you, but we live in such a harsh world that no one is exempt from receiving abuse of various kinds. If you have ever experienced unrequited love, if you have ever lent money to someone who refused to pay you back, if you have ever been unfairly passed over for a promotion, if you have ever been mistreated by someone for no good reason at all, you have been spit on.

Mr. Blind Man heard Jesus spit, yet he remained right there. This challenged me to grow in so many ways. There are times when I know I am the focus of other people's injustice, and I want to run away from their unkindness. But I can almost hear Mr. Blind Man say to me, "Don't run for cover, Soaries. Stay right there! Don't let anyone intimidate you, and don't let any circumstances discourage you. Don't let anybody's spit drive you away from the place of your blessing."

It seems as if something has happened to these latter generations that causes us to think we need to be *liked*. What I love about my grandma's generation is that they thrived even though they knew some people did not want them. They worked for rich people who let their children call them by their first names, and in my opinion when children can call senior citizens by their first names in any century or decade, that is equivalent to being spit on.

But Grandma didn't care what the rich people's children called her—she called herself a child of God. Thus, she was able to stand with her shoulders back, her head up high, looking into the hills from whence came her help (see Ps. 121:1 KJV), because no "spit" could kill her or keep her down.

We have to learn how not to crumble in the face of adversity. We have to learn how not to wither before animosity. We have to learn to stand tall amid uncertainty. The Bible teaches us that greater is He who is in you than all the spit in the world (see 1 John 4:4)!

Stay firm in what you believe. Remain resolute in your commitments and relationships. Stand strong in your resolve and determination. When you make up your mind to say yes to life's nos, don't let anyone's "spit" keep you from reaching your goal. We have to say yes and stop running anytime the Devil rears his ugly head and yells, "No!"

Once upon a time, I lived ready to pounce when people attacked me. I felt I couldn't let anyone get the best of me, so I was always poised to lash out. Many people still live that way today. Mr. Blind Man had no reason to stand there in the uncertainty of someone spitting at him and putting disgusting mud on his face. He could have left or retaliated, but he chose to do neither.

Here was a man having a bad day. He was blind. He was a beggar. He was exposed to strangers who were intrusively in his business. And while he stood next to one particular stranger on that fateful day, the stranger spit next to him.

LORD OF THE MESS

I once spoke at a convention of blind people. Everyone in the room except me was totally or partially blind. In the middle of the event, the lights went out, and I was shocked when everybody in the room gasped. How could they tell that the lights were out? But some blind people, even some who are completely blind, can sense light. So they know when it is day or night, and they know when the lights are on or off.

When Jesus put the mud over his eyes, Mr. Blind Man went from being blind to being in complete darkness. His sense that it was daytime was exchanged for pitch blackness. Talk about a no of uncertainty. I'm sure he wondered what in the world was happening to him. Still, he did not panic or depart from Jesus' presence.

The mud on his face must've felt very messy. Just as his hearing was probably extra sensitive, so likely was his sense of touch. This man already had a messy life, and here was Jesus seemingly adding to the mess by putting mud over his eyes and stealing the light.

Have you ever felt like that? Your situation is already hard and you feel you can't take one more bad thing. You pray, but instead of relief coming, things get even worse. But Mr. Blind

Man's story teaches us that there are no shortcuts in reaching our yes. We may have to go through the mess to get to it. For all you know, your miracle may be in the middle of the mud. Sometimes the thing that seems as if it's stealing your last ray of light is actually the blessing you've been pleading God to send.

When the mess comes, God is in it. God is Lord of the mess.

I like order, discipline, organization, and predictability. I am not one for surprises, and I'm certainly not fond of chaos. But some of the most significant scientific discoveries happened by accident, like the discovery of penicillin. In the same way, some of the most significant victories in the Bible came in the midst of a mess, like when the Israelites left Egypt after praying for four hundred years.

In 1 Kings 17, Elijah was in a thick mess. He had just prophesied a year-long drought to wicked King Ahab, so God told him to hide in a ravine next to a brook. Even in Elijah's time of uncertainty, God cared for him, sending black-suited waiters to bring him his dinner.

But then the brook dried up, and Elijah had to travel even farther. Lo and behold! The miracle lay farther ahead, in the humble home of a widow down in Zarephath, who fed Elijah during the famine. There is always a miracle in your mud. You only need to face the mess head on and dig in deep to unearth your miracle!

Let us consider Job. There is no other person in the Old Testament who had been as faithful to God yet who suffered as significant a loss.

He had gone from being the wealthiest man to being one of the poorest and sickest, all in a matter of moments. His children had perished, his livestock had been destroyed or stolen, his servants had died—all basically simultaneously. And if his uncertainty and pain weren't enough, his best friends kicked him when he was down. They suggested that all this had happened to Job as punishment for some sins he had committed. Even his wife had joined the "no chorus," asking him to curse God (see Job 2:9). Job was a man in a messy situation beyond our imagination. His was no mud; his was a quagmire.

Despite everything Job went through and despite all his losses, he continued to prevail and worship God through his mess. And in the end, when he had waded through his mess, God restored everything to him, and he had more children and more livestock, more servants, and more blessings than he had ever lost in the first place.

Don't give up in the mud or the mess. The blessing is hidden in it.

BEGGARS AND KINGS

Mr. Blind Man stayed right there while the disciples gossiped about him, while Jesus warmed his heart with His nonjudgmental response, while he heard this strange man proclaim to be the Light of the World, and while the same man spit into the dirt and covered his already-blind eyes with mud from His spit. Mr. Blind Man prevailed through all of it and came out victorious with his personalized, custom-made miracle.

Sixth grade was a tough year for me. Not only did my teacher predict my failure, as we have seen, but it was also in sixth grade when I first encountered some kids who I thought were my friends but who turned out to be my enemies. They were two brothers who disliked me for no apparent reason.

Have you ever had someone dislike you for no reason at all? You meet someone and on day one that person already hates you. That can't be about you, my friend. You haven't had enough time to offend anyone! That has to be about the hurt and anger that happened to that person before you ever stepped onstage.

One morning these two brothers smeared my face with blueberry pie right before the start of school. My best friend took care of them after school, if you know what I mean. But for that whole day, I was humiliated from the assault.

It was years before I was able to recognize the disguised blessing in what had happened that morning. By discovering that these brothers, who I'd previously thought were my friends, were certainly not my friends, it spared me the pain of making that discovery in subsequent grades. I had the opportunity to cross them off my list early in life and concentrate my affection on those who were genuine friends, like my friend who stood up for me that day.

When you discover that the person you trusted was really up to no good behind your back, it may feel like a mess, but it could also turn out to be the biggest blessing of your life.

Losing a job feels like a muddy mess, but it could save your life! Don't get me wrong here: we all need a source of income. But sometimes holding on to a stressful and meaningless job in a hateful environment could kill you. You may not shout "Hallelujah" while you're holding the pink slip. However, the mess of losing a job can function like the mud in Mr. Blind Man's eyes.

When I received that cancer diagnosis, it made me want to cry rather than celebrate. But after having surgery for my prostate cancer, I came to realize that the diagnosis was the best thing that could have happened. If I hadn't found out about the disease and taken steps to get rid of it, I would never have the good health I am enjoying now.

Sometimes it takes a mess and some mud to get you to your miracle.

Who had a bigger mess than Jesus? The King of Kings, Lord of Lords, Creator of the world … born of a virgin in a cold, stinking stable, along with the calves and the lambs and the kids on that wintry night in Bethlehem (see Luke 2:6–7). That was a mess!

Soon after His baptism, He was tempted by the Devil in the wilderness when He was hungry and weak after a forty-day fast (see 4:1–12). That's a mess. When He healed ten lepers, only one of them ever said thank you (see 17:11–19). That was a mess!

His family didn't understand Him (see Mark 3:21). His treasurer betrayed Him for thirty pieces of silver—not even gold (see Matt. 26:14–15). His disciples fell asleep when He asked them to watch and pray (see vv. 37–45). The religious leaders were so jealous and afraid of Him that they conspired to convict Him with false allegations from false witnesses (see vv. 57–66). That was a mess! And then Peter, His trusted disciple, denied Him three times in one night (see vv. 69–74). That was a mess!

Though Pontius Pilate said he could find no fault with Jesus, he nevertheless convicted Him of capital crimes and sentenced Him to die (see Luke 23:4–25). They made Him carry a cross that was too heavy for Him, and they nailed Him to the cross like a common thief (see Luke 23:26; John 19:17–18). They put a crown of thorns on His head and gambled for His clothes, and they gave Him vinegar to drink and speared Him in the side (see Matt. 27:28–29; John 19:23–34). That was the greatest mess of all time!

Except that it was also the vehicle for God's greatest blessing on humanity.

They mocked Jesus in His suffering, and the sun stopped shining (see Matt. 27:39–45). A disciple buried our King in his tomb and rolled a stone in front of it (see vv. 57–60). Talk about uncertainty for those who loved Him! And when it seemed it couldn't get any worse, they posted soldiers to guard His tomb (see vv. 62–66). That was a mess too! In the midst of all this mess, Jesus rose from the dead on the third day (see 28:1–6). His resurrection proved that God wields the miracle power in His hands.

The mud may be thick, but God has more power than any mud or any mess in your life.

Mr. Blind Man helped me understand that the messier my life gets, the more miraculous my life can become. The more mud life hurls into my eyes, the more blessings are hiding in the mud. The more uncertain I become, the more certain I am that my help is sure and near.

TURNING YOUR NO INTO A YES

1. Name a time of uncertainty when you were tempted to wonder whether God was really in control at that moment. Name something that happened to you and you weren't immediately certain whether it was going to end up as a blessing or a curse. Name a time when uncertainty caused (or almost caused) you to walk away from what ultimately became a blessing, miracle, or breakthrough.

2. Describe a time when someone spit on you—literally or figuratively. What did you do? What do you wish you had done? Has someone's abuse ever caused you to give up on your dream or the yes you had been wishing for? What ways might there be to reverse that decision now and go after your yes again?

3. Mr. Blind Man felt that the little light he did have had been taken from him by the mess and the mud Jesus put over his eyes. But he later realized that the thing that seemed unkind was actually the pathway to his greatest blessing. Describe a time when you felt that events had gone from bad to worse yet you later came to see that the mess and the mud were actually the things bringing God's yes to you.

6

THE NO OF THE WRONG POOL

I had full confidence that Jesus could heal my body. My confidence was rooted not only in Mr. Blind Man's story but also in the story in John 5, when Jesus healed a man by the pool of Bethesda.

When Jesus instructed Mr. Blind Man to go to the pool of Siloam, he went. The crowd was at the pool of Bethesda, yet Mr. Blind Man went alone to a pool where healing had never occurred. Sometimes God leads us to go where no one has ever gone and do what no one has ever done to fulfill His purposes.

I felt perplexed about this verse until recently: "'Go,' [Jesus] told him, 'wash in the pool of Siloam' (this word means 'Sent'). So the man went and washed, and came home seeing" (John 9:7). It disturbed me because of another event that happened in John 5, when Jesus, on His way to the temple, saw a man who had been lame for thirty-eight years. The Bible says, "After saying this, he spit on the ground, made some mud with the saliva, and put it on the man's eyes.… His neighbors and those who had formerly seen him begging asked, 'Isn't this the same man who used to sit and beg?' Some claimed that he was. Others said, 'No, he only looks like him.' But he himself insisted, 'I am the man'" (John 9:6, 8–9).

Another man had been lingering near the pool of Bethesda. People believed that the pool was stirred occasionally by an angel of God and that the first person to take a dip in the pool after it was stirred received healing. You can imagine that the disabled man was eager to get into the pool, wanting an opportunity for healing. However, even though this poor man could never make it into the pool in time because of his disability, he had remained there, hoping.

The message here, however, is not about how long the disabled man persevered or how miraculous a dip in the pool was but rather about how when Jesus showed up, the man didn't need the pool anymore. Jesus healed his infirmity and challenged him to pick up his mat and walk.

Yet the pool is so fascinating because there were crowds of people gathered around it, and, among them, a disabled man. Some scholars have suggested it wasn't an angel who came down and stirred the waters of the pool. I had the privilege of visiting the Bethesda pool when I was in Jerusalem. There is an upper pool and a lower pool, and some suggest there was a piping system that intermittently transferred water between the two pools, creating a bubbling effect as with a hot tub.

Whether it was an angel stirring or a simple bubbling of the waters, the fact remains that people gathered by the pool to claim their healing. I find it extremely unlikely that people would have gathered around a pool where nothing was happening. This pool in John 5 taught me so much about the other pool called Siloam in John 9.

DON'T FOLLOW THE HERD

When I assessed the two pools, I recognized that Mr. Blind Man was once again teaching me how to say yes when life says no. I was impressed by what he didn't do rather than by what he did do. Sometimes what we don't do is more important than what we do, and what we don't say gets us a lot further than what we do say.

In this case, the pool Mr. Blind Man chose not to visit is just as instructive as the pool where he went to wash. Had I been there listening to Jesus tell Mr. Blind Man to go wash in the pool of Siloam, I probably would have stopped listening at the word *pool* because I would have assumed Jesus was saying to go to the pool of Bethesda. Everyone knew it was the pool renowned for its healing powers! Besides, Jerusalem is only 0.35 square miles. Even though the city looms large in our minds because of its history, physically it is a tiny city.

If you went to Jerusalem today, you could still tell the size it used to be because "Old Jerusalem" is walled in apart from the new. Today we would call the Jerusalem of the Bible a neighbor-hood because it was that small.

Although the Bible doesn't specify precisely where Jesus encountered Mr. Blind Man, we do know that the disabled man's pool of Bethesda in John 5 was on the east side of Jerusalem. So wherever Jesus was in the north, south, or west, He couldn't have been more than a couple hours' stroll from the pool of Bethesda, and He could have directed Mr. Blind Man to go there.

Instead, Jesus directed him to go to the pool of Siloam, and as Mr. Blind Man obeyed the Lord's specific instructions, he ended up gaining his sight.

For our purposes, we can say that Mr. Blind Man said yes to his healing despite the no of the "wrong" pool. And by going to the pool of Siloam, he teaches us that sometimes we have to say yes to what seems counterintuitive if we want to receive what Jesus intends for us.

When I studied the process that had to accompany Mr. Blind Man's decision-making, it occurred to me that in choos-ing to go to the pool of Siloam, he decided not to follow the human "herd." The word *herd* is a metaphor for *crowd*, and I use it because in John 5 the pool of Bethesda was where the multitudes would gather. Had Mr. Blind Man adopted the herd mentality, he may have disregarded Jesus' instruction, and he could have decided to go to the pool of Bethesda instead. This would have been a mistake that could have left him without his blessing.

There are times when the group is wrong. Conventional wisdom says if everyone else is going one way and doing the same thing, then it must be right. It's difficult to break free from the "everybody is doing it" mentality, but sometimes you have to withdraw from the crowd and go in the opposite direction all by yourself.

Greatness comes to people who are willing to break away from the status quo and stand alone. People who are eager to be different. There are times when we have to look at ourselves in the mirror and say, "I'm going to do what is right, even if I'm the only one doing it." We cannot use other people's behavior as a guidance system. We need to look to Jesus for that.

Sometimes our coworkers are the crowd we have to avoid. I have worked with people who were terminated from work or penalized for doing something they knew was wrong, but they still did it because everyone else was doing it and getting away with it.

Sometimes the crowd is our family. Sometimes it's our friends or our community, and we would be wise to withdraw from the crowd that's hanging around the wrong pool.

Jesus didn't care how many people were going to the pool of Bethesda. And as the healer of the world, He also didn't care about the supposed healing powers that lay within that pool. He instructed Mr. Blind Man to go to the pool of Siloam, and the gospel says that is precisely where Mr. Blind Man went. He was not hooked on following the crowd.

Sometimes the crowd is in the church. Some religious crowds create religious fads—the religious flavor of the month, the preacher of the year, or the song of the season—and we get whipped up in these religious frenzies, and we follow the crowd.

When you think about the herd mentality, it is evident that it is ridiculous. There is a herd over here and a herd over there and a herd everywhere, and wherever the herd goes, we go too. What they say and do is what we say and do. That is no way to live!

The herd was at the pool of Bethesda, according to John 5, but to get from where he was to what God had for him, Mr. Blind Man did not follow the herd. He followed the instructions Jesus gave him.

Notice that Jesus did not promise Mr. Blind Man healing anywhere in this text. So even though he had no idea that Jesus was the Son of God and wielded the power of healing for any condition in the world, Mr. Blind Man still chose to listen to and trust this stranger.

He could base his actions only on the words Jesus had spoken. Remember, Jesus decided to meet Mr. Blind Man's needs without judging him at first glance.

This situation was not a religious encounter, and the Bible doesn't tell us whether Mr. Blind Man was a man of faith. When Jesus said, "Go … wash in the Pool of Siloam" (John 9:7), there was nothing profound about that. Those words were given as simple advice to a blind man who had mud smeared across his eyes, with no assurance of anything special to come of washing it off.

IT PAYS TO FOLLOW JESUS

When you have mud in your eyes, you don't need anyone to tell you to go and wash your face. Mr. Blind Man could have asked someone nearby to bring him a pitcher of water, and he could have washed his face right there by the street. Instead, he trudged and groped his way to Siloam because Jesus told him to. He had no reason to believe he was going to be healed, because he did not know that it was Jesus, the Messiah, who had smeared mud on his eyes.

After he was healed, he said he had been healed by someone they called Jesus (see v. 11), showing that he knew little about his benefactor, save His name.

Why, you might ask, would anyone listen to a stranger and follow His every instruction upon their first meeting? I don't know the answer to that question. It is profound that Mr. Blind Man trusted Jesus and His words without hesitation. What I do know is that without any deep, spiritual expectation and without even being a follower of Jesus, this man simply obeyed Jesus and was healed. Think about the opportunities you could be missing because you are not listening to, trusting, and following Jesus' instruction—His specific and individualized instruction prescribed just for you.

I read a marvelous book called *Jesus, CEO: Using Ancient Wisdom for Visionary Leadership* by Laurie Beth Jones. She took the teachings and lifestyle of Jesus and applied them to modern-day business practice. The book became a bestseller because it made even businesspeople who don't believe in Jesus realize how acting like Jesus helped their businesses.

I boldly declare that even if there were no afterlife, no salvation and heaven for the upright and just, and no hell for sinners, I would still follow Jesus as a person. Following Jesus means adhering to biblical principles, which make me a better student, a better parent, a better leader, a better businessman, and a better human being as a whole. Following Jesus has many benefits besides heaven.

Jesus can help people overcome problems, even if they don't consider Him their Savior. He said, "Love your enemies and pray for those who persecute you" (Matt. 5:44). That is good psychology for world peace.

Jesus asked, "Suppose one of you wants to build a tower. Won't you first sit down and estimate the cost to see if you have enough money to complete it?" (Luke 14:28). In other words, don't attempt to live without a budget. That is sound advice!

You don't have to be promised heaven to know it makes sense to live on a budget. Every Sunday I stand at the pulpit to preach, and on every platform I am given to share a message, I try to slip in a word about money management: live below your means, pay your bills on time, make sound investments, and buy life insurance.

I say that even if Jesus was not spiritual at all, had no connection to religion, and promised no streets of gold or mansions in His Father's house, it would still pay to follow Him, because the principles Jesus taught us are sound and trustworthy.

KNOW YOUR HERITAGE

We sometimes pollute Christianity by limiting Jesus to our earthly expectations of a divine quid pro quo. We even make our prayer requests conditional. "Lord, if You bless me this time, I'll serve You next time." "God, if You heal me today, I'll pay my tithe tomorrow." "God, if You give me a new job, I'll teach Sunday school once a month." We set conditions for God when, in fact, Jesus is worthy of our total obedience, not because of what we are going to get in return but because His instructions constitute the superior way to live.

Perhaps if we would stop asking God to provide for us only, if we stop focusing solely on ourselves and wondering when God is going to deliver the package we have been asking for, then perhaps we shall receive. If we just did what Jesus said, then we might discover what blessings He has for us till our cups run over.

Mr. Blind Man never asked for sight—he did not ask for anything. But he did what Jesus said, and he got what he never thought he would have. That was the key to Mr. Blind Man's blessing. Above and beyond that which we think of or ask for, God has something for us. As we focus on the words of Jesus, God, on His terms, will reveal what blessings and plans He has for us.

Mr. Blind Man did not focus on the disciples. He didn't even focus on his own healing; he merely focused on the man who had said a kind word about him. Mr. Blind Man followed

Jesus' instructions, probably thinking that it would get the mud out of his eyes, not that it would bring him sight. The actual healing for Mr. Blind Man must have been a bonus.

As we have seen, the pool of Bethesda is located on the east side of Jerusalem. The word *Bethesda* means "house of mercy." The city of Jerusalem is so small you can get to the east end from the west, north, or south without too much trouble and in relatively little time, even on foot.

The pool of Siloam was located on the south end of the city. The word *Siloam* means "sent." There was no evidence of any healing at the pool of Siloam. No previous biblical records, no reports by any witnesses had ever mentioned any form of healing occurring at this pool, whether by taking a dip in it or by praying to God on its banks. So I know what I am saying when I state that Mr. Blind Man neither followed the herd nor focused on his healing. Most importantly, he was healed because of what he did not do—he did not forget his heritage.

Heritage is the history of your ancestors. Heritage is where and how they lived, the many factors that influence where you are today. It is the culture you identify with and the traditions you live by—the food you eat and the way you dress—the lifestyle you were born into, which you pass on to your children and grandchildren. That is all a part of your heritage.

What was Mr. Blind Man's heritage? To answer this, we need to learn from Jewish people, and from all peoples of the world for that matter, that there is value in our heritage—our ethnic heritage, spiritual heritage, and national heritage.

For the rest of our country's existence, 9/11 will be etched into the fabric of the American heritage.

We at First Baptist Church of Lincoln Gardens will never forget the people who started our church in a space they rented out of a service station for four dollars every Sunday—that is a part of our heritage.

A weak people are those who turn their backs on their heritage. In 1899 James Weldon Johnson wrote in the hymn "Lift Every Voice and Sing," which says, "Keep us forever in the path, we pray ... / Lest, our hearts drunk with the wine of the world, we forget Thee."[1] Simply put, we cannot let the acquisition of worldly possessions or the attainment of affluent positions cause us to forget our humble beginnings and the God who got us through.

Some of us have forgotten our heritage. Mr. Blind Man got his breakthrough and said yes to his opportunity despite his physical and environmental roadblocks because he did not forget his heritage.

All Jewish children by the age of twelve at least vaguely understood their culture and its accompanying religious requirements. We know for sure that Mr. Blind Man was Jewish because the Pharisees spoke with him about Jesus breaking the Sabbath (see John 9:16). For this reason, we are also confident that as a child—blind or not—he must have received some instruction on Jewish culture and religion as every Jewish child did.

Now, there were three significant celebrations in Jewish culture. The first was the festival that celebrated the Passover.

The Passover was a reminder of the last plague God brought on Egypt and how the angel of death had passed over every Israelite household that was marked with the blood of a lamb, as God had instructed Moses (see Ex. 12:1–29). It is a festival Jewish people celebrate to this very day. The second celebration was Pentecost, which remembered when Moses received the law on Mount Horeb. The third grand celebration among the Jews was the Feast of Tabernacles.

Altogether, the three celebrations were Passover, Pentecost, and Tabernacles, sometimes called Sukkot. The Festival of Sukkot (also known as the Feast of Booths) ran for seven days, plus one for a sacred assembly and offering, so a total of eight days of celebration. All Jewish men were expected to make a pilgrimage to Jerusalem during this time to be in fellowship with one another at the temple and to celebrate the feast.

The booth was merely a small hut or tent that depicted the modest dwellings of the Jewish people during their forty-year journey through the wilderness. After they came to the Promised Land, they remembered that period in their history by constructing little huts or tents and living in them for the duration of the festival. The time of year for this festival was directly after the fruit harvest, so they would bring freshly harvested fruits as a thanksgiving offering to God for a bountiful supply.

Once a year, for seven days, the Jews would live inside their little huts and celebrate a season of good harvest, and they would thank God for the abundant blessings they already had. This celebration was their heritage. Even Jesus celebrated the Festival of Tabernacles and had done so as recently as John 7. It was on the last day of this celebration that He spoke these words: "Let anyone who is thirsty come to me and drink. Whoever believes in me, as Scripture has said, rivers of living water will flow from within them" (vv. 37–38).

You must be wondering by now what any of this has to do with the pool of Siloam. There is a connection that we will establish momentarily.

Mr. Blind Man was able to follow the words of Jesus, who told him to go and wash at Siloam, where, during the annual Feast of Booths, the priests would go every morning to get water for the temple to start the day's thanksgiving celebration with a water libation poured to God.[2]

When Mr. Blind Man was instructed to go to Siloam, he knew the heritage and the traditions of his people. He must have known the pool was connected to that celebration of thanksgiving. And although no miracle had ever been recorded at Siloam, nor had anyone ever been healed there—and he had not been promised healing anyway—he must have gone with the mind-set of giving thanks for what he already had and not for what he was about to receive.

I imagine he may have thought, *I know that no one has ever been healed at the pool of Siloam and no miracles have happened there, but just as the priests go down to get the water to begin the celebration of thanksgiving, even though I may still be blind and may have mud in my eyes, I have so much to be thankful for because God has been good to me. And if I never receive my sight and if I never receive another blessing in life, God has already been so good to my people and me that I have cause to go down to Siloam.*

Mr. Blind Man reported that he was able to see only after he followed Jesus' instruction and went down to wash the mud off his face (see John 9:11). If you know your heritage, then even while you are still looking for your breakthrough and rising above your specific obstacles, you will remember to choose the right pool, the pool of thanksgiving, even before you stop by the pool of healing.

SAY YES TO THE RIGHT POOL

All this may sound illogical in the general context. It makes no sense that anyone with an ailment or infirmity would not seek out the place of healing, Bethesda, but would head instead for the location of thanksgiving, Siloam.

Did it make sense for Noah to build an ark when it had never flooded before (see Gen. 6)? Did it make sense that Joseph would go from being a common slave to being the prime minister of all Egypt after spending years in jail (see Gen. 39, 41)? Did it make any sense at all that Esther, a Jewish slave girl, would be chosen from among many beautiful maidens to be queen (see Est. 2)?

It made no sense for Daniel to come out of a lions' den unscathed (see Dan. 6) and for Shadrach, Meshach, and Abednego to come out of the fiery furnace without a trace of smoke on their clothes (see Dan. 3). How can we ever explain how the Israelites crossed the Red Sea without a bridge or a boat (see Ex. 14) or how Peter could walk on water as long as he kept his eyes on Jesus (see Matt. 14)? It made no sense for Lazarus to come out of the grave walking and breathing after being dead for four days (see John 11), but it all made sense to God because He specializes in doing what makes no sense.

Don't go to Bethesda; don't just follow the crowd. Jesus says go—I'm going. Jesus says pray—I'm praying. He says give—I'm offering. Shout—and I'm shouting. It might not make any sense at all, but I once was blind, and now I see. Once I was lost, but now I'm found. I was dead, but now I'm alive, so to me it makes all the sense in the world.

Your challenge is to say yes to the right pool even when everyone else would say it's the wrong pool. God can turn what appears to be nonsense into good sense. What looks like foolishness can, by faith, propel us toward achieving our goals.

Only Jesus knows how and where He apportions healing. He said, "Whoever drinks the water I give them will never thirst. Indeed, the water I give them will become in them a spring of water welling up to eternal life" (John 4:14).

When Jesus points us toward water, it's never the "wrong" pool.

TURNING YOUR NO INTO A YES

1. Mr. Blind Man teaches us that sometimes we have to take a route that doesn't make immediate sense in order to receive what Jesus intends for us. The fact that Mr. Blind Man went to the pool of Siloam—not Bethesda— played a major role in the healing he received. Can you think of a time when a person, place, or situation you were trying to stay away from ended up providing you with a major blessing? Describe that experience. What did you gain from taking a path that you thought was counterintuitive?

2. Societal pressures promote a "follow the crowd" mentality. Think of a time when you decided to follow the crowd. What was the outcome? What disadvantages did you encounter as a result of that decision? In relation to your goals, what are the advantages of choosing to break free from the herd and be your own person?

3. Focusing solely on ourselves and wondering when God is going to deliver what we have been asking for can make it feel as if our blessing is being delayed. Have you ever felt as if your blessing has been put on hold? Consider ways you can reroute your focus, thinking, or

behavior so you position yourself for what God has in store for you. Is He instructing you to go to a place you haven't thought twice about visiting? Is He prompting you to change the focus of your prayer? Is He telling you to let go and trust in His power? Is He asking you to put your attention on other aspects of your life? What is God signaling you to do?

7

THE NO OF NEW DEVILS

When Mr. Blind Man's neighbors saw his victory, they questioned and criticized him. Mr. Blind Man probably expected them to celebrate his miracle but found himself under attack instead.

This part of his story reminds us that we must prepare for the reality that some people will not be happy with our growth or our success. But as the Bible says, "If God is for us, who can be against us?" (Rom. 8:31). With this mind-set and this promise, we can rise above any circumstance and win! When the no of opposition shows up, we can respond with the yes of determination.

At this point we have carefully analyzed the circumstances surrounding Mr. Blind Man's healing as recorded in John 9. We have considered this man and admired the fact that he never let his condition of blindness define him. He may have been blind, but the profundity of his story goes far beyond the fact that he was a blind man healed by Jesus.

We have come to respect that he still got out of bed and went into the world when he could have curled up and lamented the misfortune of his infirmity. Could you have done that?

Mr. Blind Man inspires us because when Jesus' disciples were seeking to judge him—probing into his background and trying to determine whose sin caused his blindness—he remained unfazed. He kept his cool. Would you have responded with the same sense of peace?

I am still amazed that Mr. Blind Man was undaunted by Jesus' spitting. Surely he wondered whether Jesus was spitting at him, but he waited patiently to find out what He would do. Do you think you would have handled the situation in the same way?

Bad could have turned to worse when Mr. Blind Man, who was begging but had received no money, who was talked about and nearly spit on, eventually had mud smeared over his eyes. He might have thought the mud in his eyes was an inconvenient mess, but his story suggests that sometimes there is a miracle in the middle of the mess. Perhaps he was hoping for that.

It challenged me to think that despite all that was happening to him and around him, Mr. Blind Man still obeyed Jesus' instructions and went to the pool of Siloam to wash.

God used Mr. Blind Man to teach me that there are some things only God can do for us, but there are other things that even God expects us to do for ourselves. He will wake us up in the morning, but we will have to get up out of bed on our own.

If we are going to say yes to life's new opportunities, whether to become better parents or to be more prominent and more proficient in some area of our lives, then we have to make some meaningful contribution to our upward movement. We should not expect God to do for us what we ought to do for ourselves.

We now encounter the formerly blind man as he began his new experience of living. He said yes when life was telling him no, and he went from blindness to sight.

I am happy for Mr. Blind Man. I am glad Jesus healed him, and I am thrilled that he could now welcome every new day not only with the sounds he heard with his ears but also with the sights he could see with his eyes. I am happy this man could finally look at the faces of both his friends and his enemies. Although all this happened some two thousand years ago, we still marvel at his victory that day in Jerusalem.

But not everybody is happy when you receive victory— remember that. Not everyone is going to be thrilled when you get a promotion at work. Not everyone will rejoice when your marriage is healed or when you're elected to public office. We would be wise to discern with whom we should share our good news, because sometimes the very thing we praise God for will end up being the darts people throw back at us.

It is common to encounter new "devils" when new doors open for you. That is precisely how it happened with Mr. Blind Man. Right after he washed the mud from his eyes, his new-found success introduced him to some new devils—haters who did not believe he had ever been blind, critics who accused him of being helped by a sinner, and further questions from people who had previously ignored him (see John 9:8–26).

The same man had stood on the corner of the street begging just moments before, and no one—not the children darting through the streets, not the people heading to the temple, not any of the religious leaders—had given him the time of day. But when Mr. Blind Man was promoted from being virtually invisible to being the talk of the town, the new devils suddenly appeared in protest.

This realization has caused me to be careful around people who are curious about my achievements. When you are on the street begging or when you are handicapped or when you don't have a nice car to drive, people will ignore you, perhaps because you're not achieving anything they deem to be significant. But you will draw a lot of attention the moment you make your breakthrough, and not all the attention you receive will be positive. Mr. Blind Man suddenly became the focus of everyone's interest, most of which was negative and mean.

This attention was not a celebration. Nobody slapped him on the back and said, "Mazel tov! I'm happy for you." Nobody threw a party to welcome him to the club of the sighted, nor did anyone commend him for hanging in there all those years. His was not a victory anyone celebrated.

Unfortunately, this is not unique to Mr. Blind Man. It is widespread, and it is common to feel the skepticism, criticism, and cynicism of others when you achieve success or experience a victory. Take this as a reminder that when you rise above your circumstances and reach new levels, you should expect to encounter some new devils. These devils come in all shapes and forms and will spring up out of places you would least expect.

NEIGHBORHOOD DEVILS

In John 9:8, we learn that "his neighbors and those who had formerly seen him begging"—those who knew Mr. Blind Man but ignored him daily—suddenly recognized him as a man and not just a blind man. The same people who passed him on the street and scurried by or tossed a coin or two into his bowl out of religious duty rather than empathy—all those people who stood by and heard others judge and accuse Mr. Blind Man unexpectedly approached him.

These devils now came to assess Mr. Blind Man's new condition and debate whether he was the man who used to be blind (see vv. 8–9). They said, "Isn't that the man who used to stand here begging?" One group said, "It is he." Another group challenged, "No, it can't be him." These people had not even taken enough time to identify the man who received his sight and agree on whether it was the same person they had seen before. They each had an opinion they intended for the world to hear.

That is how you know neighborhood devils. They become interested in you after they recognize an improvement in your life, but they had zero interest in you before you experienced your life improvement.

The neighborhood devils did not know the man well enough to identify him by face, yet as soon as he got his sight and started upgrading his life, all their attention was focused on him. These people represent folks who don't pay you one ounce of respect until you appear to be their equal or seem even better than them. And when you do rise, either they want to be your "friend" or they want to partner with you in business.

There are some people you think are your friends, but in reality they like you only as long as you are stressing over problems and going to bed crying. They like you when you are down and out, perhaps because it makes them feel good about themselves. They will offer encouragement and friendly advice when you are singing the blues, but as soon as you pick yourself up and change your life, they feel threatened by the smile on your face. They no longer know what role to play in your life. They can't be the hero anymore, so they make you out to be a villain.

Some years ago, the youth in our community were outraged when a police officer shot and killed an unarmed teen. When the media gathered at our church to hear my views about the matter, I invited a young man named Harry to speak at the press conference. I had met Harry at a meeting with neighborhood youth the previous night. This young man was intelligent, logical, and influential among his peers. While a few young men were determined to retaliate against the police, Harry was much more rational and tempered in his responses and quite articulate in explaining a peaceful strategy to pursue justice. I was so impressed with Harry that I asked him to address the media at our press conference. Not only did Harry impress the news reporters, but many people also believe that his leadership helped us avert a summer riot that could have crippled the city.

After the media event, I met with Harry to ask him why an articulate nineteen-year-old like him was just hanging around the neighborhood and not working or attending college. Harry described his previous challenges with high school officials who discouraged him from pursuing higher education and his inability to pay for college because of his family's financial incapacity. But he assured me that he desperately desired to attend college.

I immediately called a friend who was the president of a college in Ohio. He told me to send Harry to his school and he would make sure he was admitted and registered in time for the fall semester. Not only did Harry pack his suitcase and go to college, but he also did quite well in his classes. His greatest challenge was his relationship with the friends he left behind. Harry was the only young man from his neighborhood who had gone to college. His best friend was in jail. Every time Harry came home on a break from school, it became harder and harder to get him back to school. And his friends didn't make it any easier. They ridiculed his new school clothes, laughed at the way he was talking, and accused him of changing. He was so hurt by his friends' ridicule that he was tempted to drop out of college. We were successful in convincing him to stop returning home during breaks because the pressure from the neighborhood was so intense. Thankfully, he took our advice and graduated from Central State University. But he was almost derailed by neighborhood devils who did not want him to achieve his dream.

I don't care what neighborhood devils say about me or how hard they try to bring me down. I refuse to be perturbed. Why? Because I do not live to please the neighbors; I live to please only Jesus. I want to live not to glorify myself but only to glorify Him!

If trying to provide a good life for my family, wearing decent clothes that fit, driving a car that doesn't break down every week, pursuing another degree to be better qualified, or trying to speak proper English to escape embarrassment makes me stuck up or snotty, then I am guilty as charged.

People will try to discourage you when you suggest going back to college to get a degree. Some people will even attempt to put stumbling blocks in your way when you try to start a business. The new devils at your new level in life aim to drag you back to where you used to be rather than celebrate and help you get where you want to go. If you are ready to accept your life upgrade, be prepared for encounters with neighborhood devils.

RELIGIOUS DEVILS

The next devils Mr. Blind Man encountered were religious devils. There is nothing worse than a religious devil, hardly anything more brutal on a person's spirit than devils inside the church.

During my three decades as a pastor, I have met so many people who say they have problems with God, but a probe into their feelings reveals their problem is actually with the church. It turns out that sometimes the more they love God, the more they come to hate the church because of so many religious devils within the church structure. This was once my own story and the reason I stayed away from church for so long in my youth.

Mr. Blind Man's religious devils were the Pharisees—the Jewish religious leaders. Religious devils assume you don't have real religion because you don't do what they do and because you don't do what they tell you to do. They look down their noses at people and create segregation within the church body.

Mr. Blind Man's story reveals that even when a miracle as amazing as the healing of a man born blind occurred, the religious devils didn't question his ability to see, nor did they celebrate the power of God to give healing. They asked whether or not he was healed on the right day of the week (see vv. 13–16).

Religious devils have rules that have nothing to do with God's commandments at all. They often make people feel judged as if they are not authentic Christians because they don't follow those pointless rules.

Once I had a woman tell me that if I didn't lift my hands when I prayed, God wouldn't answer. Where do people get such ideas? There is nothing wrong with lifting your hands in prayer. The Bible talks about lifting holy hands (see 1 Tim. 2:8), but long ago in ancient Egypt, before Jesus came, the Egyptians also lifted hands when they worshipped their gods. God is not so narrow, so small-minded, so petty, so traditional, or so stylistic that He cannot or will not hear my prayer if I don't lift my hands. That sounds too ridiculous and too narrow-minded to attribute to God, who made the heavens and the earth and all that lies within.

Regardless, religious devils would have you think style is more important than substance and, if you don't do it their way, then you're not doing it God's way.

The Pharisees were religious devils who would look for a reason to create trouble only because the miracle did not happen on their terms—thus their claim that Mr. Blind Man was healed on a wrong day. When you have a breakthrough, some religious devils will try to bring you down.

FAMILY DEVILS

We can encounter so many types of devils in the course of our lives, but I am touching only on the kinds I identified through Mr. Blind Man's encounters after he received his healing. Somewhere above the religious devils and the neighborhood devils lie the worst of the bunch—family devils. These are people who are related to us biologically and people who are so close that although they may not be blood relations, we consider family.

I label them as worse than the previous two types of devils because these are the people you would expect to be in your corner and have your back no matter what. Family members are supposed to support one another and love one another through the highs and the lows, through the good and the bad. They're supposed to consider one person's achievement a victory for the whole family. If you discover a devil among this bunch, the feeling of betrayal tends to hit harder than if a deacon at your church or your next-door neighbor were to put you down.

Consider Mr. Blind Man's parents. Scripture says when his parents were asked about his healing experience, they clammed up (see John 9:18–23). The conversation with the Pharisees went something like this:

"Is this your son?"

"Yes, that's our son."

"Has he been blind from birth?"

"Yes, he was blind from birth."

"Then how is it that he can now see?"

"Hey, don't ask us. He's an adult; he can answer for himself."

Mr. Blind Man's parents were afraid they would get into trouble if they explained that Jesus had healed their son. We can assume the parents knew Jesus had healed their son because the first thing Mr. Blind Man would have done was run to find them and show them he could see. And then he would regale them with a narrative of how it had all happened.

If Mr. Blind Man had taken the time to tell his nosy neighbors and other people who had seen him, surely he must have told his parents the whole story. They likely knew every detail related to how their boy had been healed. But they took this stance because, according to the text, they were afraid they would be denied access to the synagogue if they affirmed the miracle that had taken place in their son's life.

If people you consider to be family turn their backs on you in a time of need, then they are the family devils in your life. To think that any parents would choose their high social or religious standing over acknowledging their son's breakthrough is abhorrent.

Anybody can smile in your face. Anybody can come to your birthday party or send you a lovely card in private, but the question is, "Would that person defend you when someone insults you behind your back?" If a family member cannot stand up and speak for you when you're not around, that person is a family devil.

We ought to be able to depend on those close to us, but many of them are too busy being neutral. This kind of passivity is killing many of our churches, our pastors, our families, and our children.

An engine in neutral is running, but it is not taking you anywhere. You are moving neither forward nor backward. You are just marking time. It is about time the church of Jesus, the body of Christ, got out of the neutral gear and revved up to grow the house of the Lord.

King David made it a point to reassure us in Psalm 27:10 that even if your mother and father (representing your family) forsake you, the Lord will pick you up, meaning the only dependable family is your heavenly family.

Every day God grants us an opportunity to say yes even when the devils surrounding us are saying we cannot make progress. Do not go forward with your eyes closed. Don't move ahead in your life naively, thinking everybody will be happy for you. New devils are lurking around the corner. We don't need to be paranoid about devils, but we also don't want to be surprised when people are not supportive when miracles and blessings come our way.

Remember that right after Jesus was baptized and had been in the wilderness fasting for forty days, the Devil came to tempt Him (see Luke 4). It will be the same for you. New devils will show up right after you decide to give your life to Christ or to renew your vows with your spouse or to be a more attentive parent or to go on that extended mission trip. Directly after you choose to live a life more pleasing to God, new devils will rear their ugly heads.

KNOW YOUR STORY

The opposition will always be bigger and stronger and more tactical than you have ever imagined when you make an improvement in your life. But thank God Mr. Blind Man teaches us how to deal with the new devils.

The man who was once blind dealt with his devils because he knew who he was and exactly what had happened in his life. He knew that he woke up blind that day, and he knew how he later received his sight. Mr. Blind Man knew that Jesus knew the whole truth too. This blind man knew his story better than anybody else, and no one could knock him off his truth.

Sometimes we can be intimidated into changing our testimonies. We do this because we are afraid of stigmatization and because we try to adapt to the changing times and flow with the tide.

We have all kinds of philosophy and theology around now. Eastern mysticism, astrology, yoga, atheism, and a host of others. I once read a half-page guest editorial in a newspaper written by an atheist who argued that goodness does not come from God and that people of God are not necessarily good. When we don't know our own story or God's true story, we can easily be led astray.

Many of us are dipping into multiple philosophies, perhaps to be safe from criticism. We are hedging our bets with Jesus in the morning and checking our horoscopes in the evening. Chanting among candles on Monday and attending prayer meetings on Wednesdays. We are dipping into everything, and we think we are smart—as if we are covering all our bases.

We are surrounded by cynicism and skepticism and, like Mr. Blind Man, criticism. If you listen to those philosophies long enough, you can start to believe them and come to doubt your faith. But Mr. Blind Man teaches us that when the Devil shows up, in whatever form or guise, make sure you know your story and stick with it. Regardless of how diverse, philosophical, and sophisticated media has become, we have to know what

God has done for us, and if we know our story, nothing can make us alter it.

A member of our church shared with me that her doctor had advised her to see a radiologist, but the earliest appointment she could get was in two weeks. A few days later, her condition had worsened with severe headaches and fainting spells, and she knew she would not last two weeks while waiting to get an MRI. Before the day was out, she received a call from the radiologist's office that someone had canceled and they could fit her in immediately. After the MRI they told her she had bleeding in the brain and needed immediate surgery to save her life.

Later this woman had a great testimony, and no situation or condition in her life would make her change her story. If God had not intervened with a miracle, she would have died before she was ever diagnosed.

You have to know your story. You have to be able to say, "I know what God has done for me," and no belief system or new devil should make you have doubts about who you are.

TELL YOUR STORY

Mr. Blind Man was asked three times how he got his sight, and each time his answer was consistent (see John 9:11, 15, 25): "A man named Jesus put mud on my eyes and told me to go down to the pool of Siloam; I washed the mud out of my eyes, and then I could see." Simple as that, he told his story over and over again to whoever asked for an explanation because he was sure of it.

Some of us would have said we've already told it several times so we're not going to keep talking about it. But not Mr. Blind Man. He did not tire of telling his story. If you know your testimony—whether or not it is sensational—tell somebody.

I once read a résumé that blew my mind. A man listed his undergraduate degree from Yale and a graduate degree from Harvard. And after all the accolades and achievements he could list, he declared at the end of his résumé, "I am a proud member of First Baptist Church of Lincoln Gardens." It is not about First Baptist Church or the fact that he is a Baptist at all. His résumé shows that he is proud to be affiliated with Jesus.

The psalmist said, "Let the redeemed of the LORD say so" (Ps. 107:2 KJV). The New International Version says, "Let the redeemed of the LORD tell their story." That is how you deal with your neighborhood, religious, and family devils. You tell your story. You may not know the Bible by heart, but tell your story anyway.

When someone sends me an anonymous letter, I assume it's because that person must be afraid to sign his or her name. One such letter came disguised in a birthday envelope along with all the cards on my sixtieth birthday. I was reading well wishes and receiving blessings when I found this anonymous note. The person complained that I was too self-centered and that my sermons always ended up being about me. That may be true, but my motive is pure. God has been too good for me to stand at the pulpit week after week and not tell my story. He brought me too far, lifted me too high, and healed me too thoroughly for me to keep it to myself.

Don't be too embarrassed or scared or too dignified or sophisticated to tell somebody who you are. There was a time when the church was all some of us had, and we were known by what church we attended. Now people hardly even know we're a Christian unless we speak up. So praise God and give Him the glory that you are alive today—that is testimony enough!

Mr. Blind Man remembered who gave him his story. When people asked him what had happened, he mentioned the name of Jesus (see John 9:11). He wanted everybody to know it was Jesus who put mud in his eyes. It was Jesus who sent him to that pool to wash. Jesus who healed him.

Sometimes I feel frustrated because we act as if we are proud of Jesus inside the church, but we go into neutral when we step outside. We hightail it out of the church parking lot and forget to say grace or bow our heads over lunch in a restaurant.

Mr. Blind Man didn't mind telling everyone it was Jesus who gave him his testimony. He proudly announced it was Jesus who allowed him to say yes to his healing even while life's circumstances were telling him no. And that is how you have to respond to the devils in your life—by acknowledging the name of Jesus. It is our best defense against the haters in our lives. There is still power in the name of Jesus, and demons continue to tremble at the mention of His name.

While I worked for the government some years ago, I would often be admonished before a delivery that I could talk about the Constitution, the economy, or anything for that matter, but I could not mention the name of Jesus. It's interesting that our society has come so far that you can talk about Buddha or witchcraft or meditation or demonology anywhere. The only name that seems to invoke strong annoyance is the name of Jesus.

Anytime there is intense emotion about something, there must be power or influence involved. There is healing, deliverance, and joy in the name of Jesus, and that is how you tackle the Devil. You call on the name of Jesus to fight your battles and calm your fears. He will raise you above your troubles and propel you into your future endeavors and accomplishments.

Yes, there are new devils on new levels, but the same Jesus who healed Mr. Blind Man and raised Lazarus from the dead (see John 11:43–44) can give you victory over all your devils.

TURNING YOUR NO INTO A YES

1. What meaningful contribution will you make to your life in order to ensure your upward movement? What steps will you take to help you progress toward your goals?

2. We should expect new devils whenever we reach new levels in our lives. Whether they be family, religious, or neighborhood devils,

opposition arises when people notice you are doing something better for yourself. What devils have you encountered when new doors have opened for you? What new devils can you anticipate as you continue to experience new opportunities and successes? Describe how you have dealt with opposition, or predict how you will contend with opposition as it arises.

3. What is your story? What testimony will you be able to shout out when the Devil comes knocking at your door? Finish this sentence: "I know what God has done for me because _____."

8

THE NO OF AN
UNEXPECTED FUTURE

When Jesus steps in to radically alter your life as He did with Mr. Blind Man, He not only redeems your past but also alters your future. The day Mr. Blind Man received his sight, he had no idea how much it would redirect his future. He suddenly faced new nos in the form of unexpected challenges and new decisions to make in his world of sight.

Can you relate? Sometimes we have one breakthrough in life only to encounter a new set of problems. Every time I reread John 9, I experienced more challenges in my decision-making and in my responses to life's nos. I found I had two significant beliefs to overcome.

The first had to do with race. The history of racial injustices in this country was a significant focus of my late teen years and early twenties. I had been exposed to personal indignities that made me bitter. The community where my family lived was not impoverished, but reminders about racial inequities were common throughout the community.

For instance, in our predominantly black neighborhood, the park closest to my house where we played baseball and basketball was always in disrepair. The baseball field was well worn, and there was no real upkeep at all. The grass was barely cut—and never on a regular or timely basis. We would use our parents' brooms to remove the water from the basketball courts days after it had rained because the pavement was so uneven that pockets of water would settle in. When the basketball nets were torn and dangling from the hoops, our parents would have to buy replacements with personal funds since the municipal government didn't provide much for those types of things on our side of town. Adults in the community volunteered to be the caretakers of the public tennis courts.

Our school system required that elementary students attend the school in their neighborhood. Approximately a quarter of the residents in our town were black, and we lived in four distinct neighborhoods. As a result, I attended an all-black elementary school with all white teachers and one black custodian who had a college degree. As a black man, he was not allowed to teach. I didn't feel oppressed in any way, but all of us got unusually excited when a black woman became a teacher in our school. We almost had not noticed that all the teachers were white until she arrived! What we did notice was that there were always student names we didn't recognize written in our books on the first day of school.

When we got to junior high, we met some of the students whose names had been in our books. There were only two junior high schools, and they were necessarily integrated. It was there that we realized that the white students had received the books when they were new and the black students had received the books after they were used and had become worn.

All these realities came to a head on April 4, 1968, while I was a junior in high school. Sadly my grandmother informed me that Martin Luther King Jr. had been assassinated. That was the day I decided to spend the rest of my life fighting injustice as Dr. King did. But the lesson I had to learn was that a passion for justice was insufficient to help me make decisions in response to personal challenges in my life. I also had to outgrow the belief that I could not do something positive with my life until all injustice was eliminated.

I am still committed to addressing injustice wherever I find it. I came to understand that I can pursue my calling and my destiny even while injustice lurks throughout the world. In fact, failure to do so would limit my ability to bring value to my work. For instance, at one time I had become so active in civic affairs and social uplift that I had ignored my own need to be financially healthy. I lived the first part of my adult life as a public activist whose personal finances were an embarrassment.

The ideas that I needed to pay my bills on time, live within my means, and save money for emergencies were not important to me. I never felt hypocritical attending community improvement meetings and going home to calls from bill collectors.

Involvement in efforts to repair all the ills of the nation and the world could not be a substitute for being a responsible adult and handling my own business. We cannot blame personal irresponsibility on institutional and systemic failures no matter how glaring they are.

This all came to a head for me when my paternal grandmother died. My dad's mother was born at the turn of the twentieth century and became a seamstress as a young woman. She married a Jamaican immigrant, and after they had six children, my grandfather had a stroke and was confined to a wheelchair until the day he died. That made my grandmother the breadwinner in her house. She had to raise six children while caring for her handicapped husband—all while earning a living sewing dresses.

When my grandmother died, she owned three debt-free houses. My uncle and I inherited one of those houses, making it the very first house I would own. As I stood at her gravesite and watched her casket lowered into the ground, I promised myself that I would change the way I was living. Here was a black woman, with no financial support from a husband, living in New York without all the rights that were enacted late in her life, who owned real estate and left a legacy of wealth transfer to her children and her grandson. Here I was with an education, civil rights, and a closet full of newspaper clippings—but nothing to leave behind but a pile of credit card bills and other debts.

My grandmother, Carrie L. Soaries, did not have the benefit of societal fairness, but she did not allow that to stop her from pursuing what was best for her family and herself. She never saw herself as a victim, so she never behaved like one.

My second area of growth had to do with overreliance on God. After I became a Christian, I was convinced that God would not allow me to experience failure. The biblical stories about God's miraculous power in both the Old and the New Testaments inspired me on a daily basis, and the more focus I gave to God's power, the more confident I became that God would come through for me. After all, God had miraculously saved my life when drug dealers kidnapped me and took me to a vacant lot to shoot me at age nineteen.

When I arrived at college as a freshman, one of my classmates died on the first day of school because of a drug overdose. My friends and I agreed that a drug culture could not flourish, and we became the dominant anti-drug force on our campus. We found the student who had provided the drugs to the victim, told him that his drug selling was not welcome on our campus, and bought him a one-way ticket to fly back to his hometown. Our anti-drug activities became a threat to the local dealers. I will describe the details a little later, but the key takeaway here is that since God delivered me from that ordeal and I didn't even pray to be delivered, I believed that God could and would handle all my troubles once I became a Christian and a minister of the gospel.

That confidence in God caused me to have the kind of complacency that defied the words of James, who said that "faith by itself, if it is not accompanied by action, is dead" (James 2:17). I had "grown" spiritually and was placing all my faith in God. So I expected God to ensure my financial security without me saving money. I believed God would keep me healthy without any effort on my part toward an exercise regimen or healthy food. I was confident that God would grow my church without me having a strategy for church growth and that God would heal my body when I was diagnosed with cancer.

I do believe God can perform any deed He decides to perform and can create whatever change He desires in an instant. However, that belief had the effect of exempting me from personal responsibility, and I needed to outgrow my dependence on it. Mr. Blind Man taught me conclusively that it is the combination of our efforts and God's power that results in changing outcomes. And the first level of our effort has more to do with "the renewing of your mind" (Rom. 12:2) than with any physical task. It is how we look at the world, our lives, our options, and our responsibilities that determines our responses to the inevitable nos we experience in life.

I concluded that I could not sit back and wait for God and attribute that posture to faith. I realized that I had to look my no in the eye and proceed toward my yes with determination even though I could not see the outcome. Today my motto is "Faith in Action!" One day in Mr. Blind Man's life changed my life for the rest of my days. And that one chapter of the Bible made the entire Bible make sense to me.

So as I read John 9, I watched this man wake up and choose to enroll in the course of a new day by getting moving. He resisted the temptation of surrendering to his infirmity and said yes to the possibilities of a brand-new day. Mr. Blind Man got up and washed his face, brushed his teeth, and prepared himself as best he could to meet the public outside his house. At this point it was just another ordinary day. But perhaps he understood that no day is just another average day. Every day is a gift from God. And since no day is a repeat of any other, saying yes to a new day means treating every day as special.

I have been driving the same make, model, and color automobile for many years. From the outside it may appear that I haven't changed cars at all. But every time I change cars, there are always a couple of critical features in the new car that make it distinctly different from the previous car. Every new day functions the same way. Today may look exactly like yesterday, but there is always something new that makes it different from the day before. God's mercies are new every morning (see Lam. 3:22–23), and the very fact that we awaken to a new day means that God has extended a new portion of mercy and treated us better than we deserve. Whatever is wrong in our lives can be subordinated to our gratitude for this profound gift from God.

YES BEHAVIOR

Mr. Blind Man left his house alone. He never waited for the assistance or the affirmation of others. He walked out of his house unassisted and unaided by friends or family. He left home determined to accomplish something all by himself. His yes behavior has encouraged me when I have felt alone in many of my pursuits.

I once expressed my belief to an audience that consumer debt was having a more significant negative impact on black Americans than racism. Before even hearing my explanation, many people in the audience were visibly uncomfortable with my perspective. Soon they were joined by a popular Ivy League professor who was a member of the panel at this event. Thankfully, Mr. Blind Man had inspired me to understand the power of proceeding even while being alone.

Mr. Blind Man stood in silence while Jesus' disciples accused him of being either a sinner or the child of sinners. When I was a kid, if anyone ever said anything negative about someone's parents—especially someone's mother—they were fighting words. If someone insulted you, the most hurtful words you could utter in response were "Your mama!" But Mr. Blind Man never said a word. Had he gotten into a debate with these men, he could have missed the miracle that Jesus had waiting for him.

Even when Jesus spit and Mr. Blind Man didn't know whether the saliva was meant for him, he stood in his place.

When Jesus smeared mud on his eyes, he waited for Jesus' instructions. And when the instructions made no sense, he followed them anyway and went to a pool where no one had ever been healed.

Before I got to know Mr. Blind Man well, my dad, who was my pastor and my mentor, had died. I had reached a point in my life when I wasn't sure whether there was any more for me to accomplish. If there was, I couldn't see what it was. The cancer in my body was screaming a loud no, and there were other whispers of no throughout my circumstances. I needed someone who was qualified to advise me holistically. I needed a role model who understood what it was like to be me. I wanted to find someone who also couldn't see a prosperous future until he had a meaningful, transformative encounter with Jesus. I never found a physical mentor or counselor. Mr. Blind Man became that for me instead, and God used him to bless and change my life. He said yes to his no experiences, obeyed Jesus' instructions, and received his sight.

What a day in his life! What a change in one day. He would now see the sun set in the west and rise in the east for the first time. He could now use candles to light his house when no one else was there because now he too could see. He could now walk much faster down the crowded streets of the city and stop along the way to look at the goods for sale in the shops. He could now see people coming his way from a distance and greet them from afar. His future suddenly appeared bright and full of promise.

It all happened in one day. Mr. Blind Man had awakened on this day as he had every other day of his life. His only plans were to do what he always did—sit on the street and beg. Now not only could he see, but his entire life had also been turned upside down. His most significant no—blindness—had become a major yes—sight. He hadn't planned this development. As far as we can know, he had no dream of being able to see. His lifelong no had become a divinely bestowed yes, and then he discovered the challenge of living with his sight.

I often say that success can be more challenging than failure. As long as this man was blind, he had every right in the world to behave like a blind man. No one would condemn him for begging—he was blind. No one expected him to give to the poor—he was poor himself. He had mastered the art of living blind. There was no reason for him to have any plans or expectations based on gaining sight because blind people receiving their sight was unheard of.

Even if he had heard of Him, Mr. Blind Man was not looking for Jesus the way others had searched for Jesus. The woman who was hemorrhaging pushed through the crowded streets to get to Jesus (see Luke 8:43–48). Four men took their paralyzed friend to see Jesus, and when they arrived where He was, it was so crowded that they climbed on top of the house and lowered their friend through the roof to get him close to Jesus (see Mark 2:1–5). A Roman centurion found Jesus to request that He heal his servant who was sick in his home (see Matt. 8:5–13). But Mr. Blind Man wasn't looking for Jesus that day.

THE RESPONSIBILITY OF YES

Many different words could be used to describe this kind of encounter depending on a person's theology and worldview. *Luck. Serendipity. Chance. Coincidence. Providence.* Whatever word you might use, the outcome doesn't change: a man now had to restructure his entire life based on an encounter with Jesus that changed his no into yes.

Mr. Blind Man's first change was to stop begging. As long as he was blind, he could justifiably depend on others to provide for him. Now that he could see, it was going to be unreasonable for him to be dependent on the benevolence of others. The first question his neighbors asked after he received his sight was "Isn't this the same man who *used to* sit and beg?" (John 9:8). I put *used to* in italics to emphasize the fact that he was no longer begging.

Mr. Blind Man could have been so attached to his lifestyle of begging that he continued to beg after he received his sight. But he was now free from the restrictions that the no of blindness had imposed on him. That freedom came with responsibility. It is true he didn't know he would be healed that day, but immediately upon being healed, the onus was on him to act healed. Now his future looked radically different and challenging.

After I became New Jersey secretary of state, I had trouble accepting the reality of my position. It was certainly an unexpected future for me. First and foremost, this position was one that was appointed by the governor, and I had not supported the governor politically. Further, this position is very prestigious, as it is one of the three executive positions required by the state constitution. Typically a governor would appoint a prominent member of his or her political party to such a position. I was a registered independent, as I am today. Until then a black man had never held one of these offices in the state of New Jersey.

When I was much younger, I had a few "scrapes" with the law that would certainly be noticed during my background check. In addition to all that, I had never held a government job in my life. I had worked in civil rights, nonprofit, and church organizations, but the governor insisted, and I was sworn in as New Jersey's thirtieth secretary of state. My name was on the door of the first office on the left as you entered the state capitol. A state trooper came to my house every day to drive me to the capitol and anywhere else I went. I had an office as large as the sanctuary of my first church. It was surreal. A few days after I began serving, I sat behind my huge desk and called my wife to tell her that I didn't feel as if I was indeed the secretary of state. Her response was, "Well, you are the secretary of state, and you'd better act like it!"

When our previous no turns into a present yes, it behooves us to begin acting as if we have what we have and we are who we are. Suppose the man Jesus healed in John 5, who had been an invalid for thirty-eight years, went back and sat by the pool after he had been healed. Suppose the woman who was healed by touching the hem of Jesus' robe kept holding His robe after she was healed (see Luke 8:43–48). It would have been pre-posterous for Lazarus to remain in the tomb after Jesus raised him from the dead (see John 11:43–44). Perhaps that's why Jesus said more than "Lazarus." It was sufficient to call Lazarus's name to bring him back to life, but after Jesus said, "Lazarus," He said, "Come out!" (v. 43). Why would Jesus bless someone with a miracle only to have that person live as he or she did before the miracle?

Mr. Blind Man now had to act as if he had sight. Thank God he did! He was the man who used to beg but no longer needed to.

When our no in life becomes a yes, we have to be ready to accept the responsibility that comes along with yes. God has blessed so many people with yeses in our modern world. Billions of people have the right to vote for their government leaders in democratic countries. Billions of people have access to modern conveniences that make life easier. We now commu-nicate globally using technologies that were considered science fiction not long ago, and information about almost anything is just a click away for billions of people on the planet. God has allowed human innovation to develop methods of overcoming barriers to nearly anything we have the will to conquer.

Yet a large segment of the world still lives in substandard conditions. Many people live with limited access to clean water, exposure to diseases, and debilitating poverty. Many endure despots and dictators as leaders and the denial of human rights that others take for granted. Mr. Blind Man didn't need to beg anymore. But he was also now in a position to help those who remained blind and those who begged for a living as he had once done. If we are going to act as if we have enjoyed the benefit of God turning our no into a yes, we will remember to love and serve those whose no persists and whose yes is elusive.

"From everyone who has been given much, much will be demanded; and from the one who has been entrusted with much, much more will be asked" (Luke 12:48).

CELEBRATE THE PROCESS

As you can imagine, Mr. Blind Man's sight created a significant stir in the neighborhood. The citizens disagreed about whether or not the man who could now see was the same man who had been blind. And unlike his silence in response to the criticism of Jesus' disciples, Mr. Blind Man spoke up. Notice the difference: he refused to argue with people who had already come to their conclusions—but he spoke up when it was time to give his testimony. When he spoke, he described the entire process and not just the results of the process. Hear his testimony: "The man they call Jesus made some mud and put it on my eyes. He told me to go to Siloam and wash. So I went and washed, and then I could see" (John 9:11).

He described what both he and Jesus had done. These are the words that grabbed my attention and attached me to this miracle. My original purpose for studying this text was to capture the reality of what Jesus could do for me. But this man changed my understanding by helping me realize that getting from life's no to God's possible yes is a process that involves me.

The epic story of God's deliverance of His people in the book of Exodus is one of both triumph and tragedy. When God used Moses to lead the freedom march of the children of Israel, they had been praying for four hundred years. They had four hundred years of no, and many of them had probably concluded that their no of slavery was a permanent one. Then God raised a leader to represent the yes of His future for them, yet many of them were unprepared for the unexpected future that lay ahead. They had trouble abandoning the ways of Egypt. It took weeks to get Israel out of Egypt and years to get Egypt out of Israel! The people failed to see that making it to the land that God had promised their father Abraham would be the result of a process and not just one big miracle. And their behavior, their choices, their obedience, their values, and their faith would all be critical factors in the process.

Jesus could have merely spoken to Mr. Blind Man's eyes, and they could have been healed just as He spoke healing for the centurion's servant in Matthew 8. But more often than not, God calls us into a process that requires a series of significant yeses before culminating in our major yes. If we are honest, when our no becomes yes, we will testify and explain the entire process to make sure we tell all the aspects of our change. When we celebrate, we should celebrate the whole process and thank God for every part of our experience.

I mentioned being kidnapped by drug dealers earlier. Yes, God miraculously delivered me. I had been leading an anti-drug crusade on my college campus. Some students had decided they were going to finance their college education by selling drugs to other students. On the first day of classes, a freshman died of an overdose. A few of my friends and I decided that we could not allow our campus to become drug headquarters. We sponsored anti-drug rallies and distributed anti-drug materials.

One night during our anti-drug campaign, we went to a drug dealer's apartment, and while my friends distracted the young man, I found his drugs and flushed them down the toilet. That was not a wise thing to do. A couple of weeks later, he and a few of his friends burst into my dormitory room at 5:30 a.m. with guns pointed at me. They ordered me to follow them outside and into the back seat of a two-door car. They then drove for about fifteen minutes to a vacant lot off a state highway. From there we could see a police car parked on the highway, and apparently, the policeman inside the vehicle could see us too. My abductors realized this, returned to the main road, and drove farther south until the police pulled us over. The officer asked what we were doing in that area and gave the driver a ticket for driving without registration.

My kidnappers had assured me they would shoot both the officer and me if I said anything when he stopped us. I remained quiet, but that traffic stop saved my life.

The driver panicked because he could now be identi-fied since he had received a ticket. They decided to take me to an apartment in a nearby city to regroup and check with the people for whom they were working. While they held me in the apartment, their colleagues informed them by phone that the FBI was looking for me because the news media had reported my abduction. They were ordered to release me and leave the country. They drove me to the campus of Princeton University and released me right across the street from where I would later attend seminary to prepare for pastoral ministry. After being released, I took the bus back to my campus, which was less than twenty miles north of Princeton.

I understand that we have important work to do to improve police/community relations, especially in minority communi-ties. But I will never be one to believe that all police are bad. Whenever I tell that story, I want people to hear how a white policeman saved this black boy's life!

Mr. Blind Man named Jesus as the one responsible for his sight. Not only were his eyes opened to see, but his experience also caused him to conclude that Jesus was the Son of Man (see John 9:35–38). Not only had Jesus proved He was the solution for this man's issue, but God also sent Jesus to be the fulfillment for which Mr. Blind Man's community had been waiting. God revealed, through Jesus, His willingness and ability to transform the entire nation into "yes" people. Jesus asked the man whether he believed in the Son of Man (see v. 35). This was the critical question because God was revealing His desire for every living creature through this one man.

There are different views about the exact meaning of this phrase *Son of Man*. Without getting into the theological and Christological debate, it is clear Mr. Blind Man believed it had some messianic and divine significance, because after he said he believed, he worshipped Jesus (see v. 38). The man attributed his healing to the power of God through Jesus. He said any change that drastic had to have come from a divine source (see vv. 32–33). Jesus' deeds refuted the speculation that he was a sinner.

We may not know the date that our no will turn to yes, but at the very least we should be prepared at any time to share the good news about what God has done. Great parents raised me; I have attended wonderful schools. I have made some very strategic connections, and I have been blessed with good friends. But it has been the power of God through Jesus Christ that has turned my life's no responses into yes!

What does that really mean? It means I have accepted Jesus' standards for my life instead of allowing the changes in culture to establish my boundaries. It means my belief in the presence of God has given me a sense of accountability that I otherwise would not have. In a culture that has added the commandment "Thou shalt not get caught," my belief that God sees and knows everything has protected me from the temptation of believing that I can do whatever I can get away with.

It means God's Spirit—the Holy Spirit—actually gives me the ability to accomplish deeds I couldn't do without help from a power greater than myself. And it means I am no longer plagued or embarrassed by the guilt I used to have for mistakes I made in my past. Jesus cleared my record of all misdeeds. No one can hold them against me.

None of life's nos can be God's punishment for past mistakes since Jesus already absorbed my punishment when He died on the cross. I may experience physical consequences for mistakes I have made, but they are not divine punishment that should make me feel guilty. Jesus didn't die to allow me to drive above the speed limit without getting a speeding ticket. Jesus died to protect me from being punished for my sins against God that would disqualify me from living in heaven when I die. That freedom allows me to function, dream, lead, create, and share freely because I am connected to a plan for humanity that was created by the same God who created humanity.

God could have allowed me to be killed by those drug dealers, which would have been an ultimate no of an unexpected future. Yet in His mercy He made a way of escape so I could live the future He had planned for me. That is why I worship God. He deserves all the praise for my life!

TURNING YOUR NO INTO A YES

1. Describe a time when you experienced a breakthrough in your life only to encounter a new set of problems. How did you handle

the situation? Can you use past setbacks to arm yourself for future obstacles? Describe how you will do that. What lessons did you take away from life's setbacks?

2. Think about a time when the odds were stacked against you. How did you react? Did you demonstrate yes behavior? What yes behavior will you commit to in preparation for future obstacles?

3. Are you prepared to accept the responsibility of your life's next yes? What habits will you equip yourself with to help you get the most out of the blessings you receive? Don't forget to celebrate the whole process! Continually give God thanks for the experience.

9

THE NO OF MISINTERPRETED SIGNS

In June 1990 I applied for a job to become the next pastor of First Baptist Church of Lincoln Gardens in Somerset, New Jersey. I didn't describe it this way at the time, but between sending in my résumé and serving my first day on the job four months later, all I could hear was the word *no*!

When I consider all the ways my relationship with this church has unfolded, I now understand that the principles I learned from Mr. Blind Man had been inculcated into my life without my ever realizing it. It is profound because I didn't fully comprehend the lesson I was being exposed to until twenty years into my pastorate.

Had I not said yes when the church seemed to be saying no to me—my experience, the life of my family, the growth and impact of the church, and the status of the community surrounding the church would all be different from what they are today. I am sure you also have had experiences like this in your life. Sometimes you aren't aware of the lesson you needed to take away from the experience until days, months, or maybe even years after the situation happened.

When I arrived at First Baptist Church of Lincoln Gardens in November 1990, all I could see was a great big no. The state the church was in made it difficult for me to envision any kind of progress. I was blind to any of the possibilities for meaningful impact and tremendous growth that lay ahead. At that time I thought there was no way I would be called to lead the congregation, and if I was, I would not last more than six months in the church.

The very first no was the location of the church.

Because of my background in activism and social change, it was important for me to become familiar with local government officials and policymakers. In an effort to identify and connect with the mayor of Somerset, I discovered that Somerset did not have a mayor. It was neither a town nor a city. It had a zip code, but I quickly learned that Somerset was one of a few sections within Franklin Township. Though I considered myself as having a global ministry, I found myself the pastor of a church in a place that wasn't even an actual town or city.

As I was processing this reality, I began to look for the location of Lincoln Gardens. I could not find it, and after an extensive search, I discovered that the neighboring town had a small apartment complex called Lincoln Gardens. I am still not sure how the church determined that it was "of" Lincoln Gardens, but this naming simply exacerbated my frustration with being the pastor of this church. I understood why the church did not simply call itself "First Baptist Church." But what kind of church, I wondered, would name itself after a small apartment complex?

When racial segregation was the dominant culture in Southern states, black Baptists would name almost all their First Baptist Churches by adding a descriptor or place name behind it. That was because there was usually a church owned by members of the majority community that was the First Baptist Church of that community. In many instances, black churches that were not in proximity to white churches still added something to their name because of social conditioning. For example, First Baptist Church in Fort Lauderdale, Florida, is First Baptist Church. Period. Around the corner from that church is First Baptist Church Piney Grove. That was the "colored" First Baptist.

In our case, there was (and still is) a First Baptist Church in the neighboring city of New Brunswick. Although our church is in a different town and different county, it was probably deemed "appropriate" to add the "of Lincoln Gardens" to our name to distinguish the church from the other First Baptist, which is only two miles away, albeit in a different community.

The other factor that created some discomfort was the church's lack of an organizational infrastructure and modern programming. The members of the church were the warmest and friendliest I had met in years. My family and I could not have felt more welcomed by the congregation.

First Baptist Church of Lincoln Gardens had two vibrant worship services every Sunday, a plethora of auxiliaries including nine choirs, and it functioned as the center of community life even in a northern state where religious observance had begun to wane significantly. It was a highly spirited, very active body of believers.

When I introduced the need for the church to secure the services of an accounting firm to conduct an audit of the church's financial records, many of the members responded by defending the integrity of the man who had been their treasurer for many years. The church owned hundreds of thousands of dollars in securities, and no one was managing the assets. But the idea that a church should function as a business was foreign to some and offensive to others. Many Christians believe the church is purely spiritual, and the idea of requiring budgets, cash flow projections, balance sheets, and external financial audits is just too "worldly" and "corporate."

The people at Lincoln Gardens were wonderful, but the business aspects of the church frightened me even before my final interview. After preaching as a candidate to become the third pastor of the church, the search committee scheduled my interview. To prepare for it, I wanted to learn as much about the church as possible. I contacted my liaison to the committee and requested copies of the constitution, budget, history, and strategic plan. They had none of these documents. I could not believe that a church of fifty-two years—with a healthy membership and educated leaders—was functioning without any of these corporate documents.

Upon hearing this news, I decided to withdraw from the candidacy for the position of pastor. After all, I had applied only because my mentor, Dr. Samuel D. Proctor, had recommended me to them and them to me. My decision to withdraw was a response to what I thought was a no. I would later realize it was a misinterpreted warning sign, because it was actually an invitation.

We have to be careful not to jump to the conclusion that some situations, circumstances, or even people are nos. Not only are certain opportunities embedded in what looks like a no, but I have also learned that a real no can in fact be a yes. Let's not forget Mr. Blind Man. In a sense, his nos in John 9 were actually opportunities:

- When Jesus' disciples refused to take him seriously, he chose not to waste time trying to get close to people who could not help him. Their judgmental disposition was a blessing—a yes embedded in a no.
- When Jesus sent Mr. Blind Man to the pool of Siloam instead of the pool of Bethesda, he experienced the yes of his healing that was embedded in the no of Bethesda.

- The no of disbelief by the religious leaders actually facilitated the yes of Mr. Blind Man's belief in and acceptance of Jesus.

Depending on our perspective, we could believe that life is saying no when in fact the appearance of a no can be the presence of opportunity.

CHOOSE TO SEE OPPORTUNITY

A company called HomeVestors of America specializes in buying houses that people want to sell quickly. I have never interacted or done business with this company, but I am inspired by the way they brand their company. Another name for their company is We Buy Ugly Houses.[1] This intrigues me because their brand suggests that they see value and potential in houses that other people perceive to be burdens or problems. In other words, they believe a house that is saying no to the current owner is a house that says yes to them!

What appears to be a no can actually be more of a blessing when properly understood. Suppose Mr. Blind Man had asked Jesus for permission to go to the pool of Bethesda and Jesus had said yes. And suppose Mr. Blind Man had gone to that pool only to discover the crowd was so large and the healing occurred only when the angel came to stir the water. What if he had to be put on a waiting list for his healing?

In other words, sometimes a no to one thing could be a yes to something better. Sometimes when life says no, God is actually saying yes. That is what happened to me at First Baptist, but I needed my mentor to help me see my no as an opportunity. And I needed Mr. Blind Man to help me understand what I had come to see.

Dr. Proctor was a prominent Baptist minister in America. He had been the president of two colleges, an associate director of the Peace Corps, a tenured professor at Rutgers University, and senior pastor at the renowned and historic Abyssinian Baptist Church in Harlem, New York.

I had first met Dr. Proctor in the 1970s when I worked for civil rights activist and aide to Martin Luther King Jr., Rev. Jesse Jackson, who had been a student at North Carolina A&T State University while Dr. Proctor was the president. We met again while I was pursuing my master of divinity degree at Princeton Theological Seminary in Princeton, New Jersey.

Dr. Proctor saw potential in me as a preacher at Princeton, and when I graduated, he invited me to an invitation-only doctoral program at the United Theological Seminary in Dayton, Ohio.

By the time First Baptist Church of Lincoln Gardens began their search for a new pastor, I had been in the doctoral program as a "Proctor Fellow" for one academic year. When the church sought Dr. Proctor's advice concerning their search, he felt I was the one for them.

I knew how strongly Dr. Proctor felt about me being the pastor of a large church in the town where he lived, and I knew how genuine he was about his desire to help me with my career. Therefore, I felt I had to break the news in person that I had decided to withdraw my name from consideration by this church.

A couple of weeks before my scheduled interview, I arranged to have lunch with Dr. Proctor. During lunch I thanked him for the referral and told him I was going to withdraw from the process. I explained all my trepidation about the church. I lamented that the church had no constitution, no budget, no strategic plan, and no written history.

He stared at me and said, "If they had all of that, they wouldn't need you!" He could have stopped right there. Here I was reenacting my own version of the Old Testament prophet Jonah, who did not want to accept God's assignment to an undesirable place (see Jon. 1). My mentor had to remind me of my calling and my commitment to serve where I was needed.

But he did not stop with that very humbling rebuke. He told me that if ministers with my training and experience were not willing to serve in churches like First Baptist Church of Lincoln Gardens, then the future of all churches was in jeopardy—especially black churches that had been so critical for the survival of black people.

He closed his rebuke by stating that this little church in Somerset could become one of the most influential churches in America with the right leadership. At that point I thought someone had slipped something intoxicating into his iced tea and he was delusional. But his additional remark was that he would kick me out of his doctoral program if I withdrew.

The case was closed, and the rest is history!

I have no idea who the influences were in Mr. Blind Man's life. I just find it so hard to believe that he had learned all these dos and don'ts without having a role model—a mentor to inspire, instruct, and guide him. I wonder whether someone caused him to believe that the no of blindness should not be like a prison guard keeping him locked into a marginal existence.

If we want to avoid misinterpreting signs, we would be wise to find three types of mentors:

1. Biblical mentors whose life experiences function as both guidance and warning for our lives.

2. Historical mentors whose stories inspire us because they were able to overcome similar challenges to the ones we face.

3. Physical mentors who can walk with us, pray with us, hold us accountable, advise us, and encourage us.

Even though I followed through with pursuing the position, the prospect of becoming the pastor of this church continued to scream no at me.

After my interview I was invited to preach for a second time on a Sunday morning. The committee decided to present my name to the congregation and have them decide whom to select as the next pastor. Because the church had never done this before (the first pastor was the founder, and the second pastor had served under him), the church had no precedent for how to make the decision. And because the church had no constitution or bylaws, the process was not governed by any formally established guidelines. What ensued was an ad hoc process that proved to be flawed and ultimately problematic.

Much to the surprise of many, I received the most votes. The election ended with many disgruntled members, and the deacon chairman called to tell me that I had been elected pastor. At the time I was unaware of the issues and uproar this decision-making had caused.

Because I was elected pastor, the next step was for the church to send me the official "letter of call." About one week went by, and no letter arrived at my home. I lived only a thirty-minute drive from the church, and normal mail would have reached my home within two days. I could hear the word *no* ringing in my ears!

PATIENCE IS KEY

Waiting is almost always interpreted as a no, despite the fact that the apostle Paul described patience as one of the fruit of the Holy Spirit (see Gal. 5:22). We don't like to wait even though the prophet Isaiah made waiting sound so enriching and noble: "Those who hope in the LORD will renew their strength. They will soar on wings like eagles; they will run and not grow weary, they will walk and not be faint" (Isa. 40:31).

Yet people of faith are not necessarily any more inclined to wait than people without faith in God. We are a fast-paced, highly mechanized world, and when we push a button or click a link, we expect something to happen and happen fast. When things do not happen fast, too often we interpret the wait as a no.

But Mr. Blind Man went through a process, and his healing was not instant. He had to wait for the dialogue among Jesus and His disciples to end, he had to wait until Jesus smeared mud on his eyes, and he had to travel to the pool. It seems like a quick event because it takes only a few minutes to read John 9. But for Mr. Blind Man, until it was over, this may have felt like the longest day of his life. He could have justifiably concluded that this process was too lengthy for an outcome that was not even conceivable. But we can see that waiting was not a no.

I grew to learn that the delay in hearing from this great church was not a no, even though the nos just kept coming. The search committee and the trustees had constructed a compensation proposal for the new pastor that was presented after I had been selected. That compensation was my next no, and I was prepared to answer by saying no. But God had matured me by this time in my life, and my answer was much more refined than it would have been twenty years prior.

Despite the no that was ringing in my inner ears, I responded in a much more dignified way than they may have expected. When they asked me to accept an 80 percent pay reduction to become their pastor, my first answer was that I could live *with* that compensation but I could not live on it. I assured them that I would accept the compensation as long as there was no prohibition against my having outside sources of income, including speaking and teaching.

That indeed was more acceptable to all of us than negotiating for a more generous compensation package. It was the second part of my answer that surprised them. I told them that a church is accountable to God for compensating their staff. Therefore, if that was the best the church could do for the pastor, God would be pleased and I would accept it. If they could do better but refused, that would be between them and God and would not be my problem.

I assured them I would never ask the church for a raise or any other financial support. I closed by stating if God sent me to be their pastor, I would have to accept the call even if they could not afford to pay me at all. And if God had not sent me, there would be no amount of money that would keep me there. I think they were surprised by my words, and those men became my strongest supporters and tremendous friends to my family and me.

I now know that my journey of assuming the position I have held for most of my adult life was replete with nos all the way to the job—and in many instances on the job. Regardless, I thank God for the fact that when I could not see any possibility of this relationship becoming what it has, God gave me the faith to say yes. When it seemed as if people hated me when they didn't even know me and spread untruths about me to thwart my candidacy, I am grateful to God that my response to their no was yes.

I realized many years later that people were spitting all around me, but I hung in there and remained close to my destiny just as Mr. Blind Man did. I had been hoping to leverage my experience and exposure to assume a significant position in some major church in a big city like Washington, DC; New York City; Atlanta; Dallas; or Los Angeles. But I said yes to a small section of a small town—as if Somerset became my Siloam. And as the church began to grow and become an even more influential institution than it had been, new devils appeared with new nos that required new yeses. I never understood all the seemingly disconnected strangeness and struggles until John 9 made them so very clear.

Today this little church in this small place has received global attention. In 2010 the CNN documentary *Almighty Debt: A Black in America Special* was viewed by millions of people who got to see a black church helping people find financial freedom in the middle of a global financial crisis.[2] And this nameless man who had been born blind mentored me, a skeptical pastor who thought he was hearing no but was actually receiving a divine yes.

I really should not have needed the man born blind to teach me that. I could have learned it from Jesus. After all, the innkeeper said no to His delivery, Herod said no to His birth, His cousin initially said no to His baptism, the religious leaders said no to His teaching, His disciples said no to His death, and death said no to His life. But He said yes to His mission, and God said yes to His victory. When life says no, Jesus says yes. That is all we need.

TURNING YOUR NO INTO A YES

1. Think of a time when you didn't know the lesson you needed to take away from an experience until days, months, or years after it happened. Describe how these life lessons affected you.

2. There are opportunities embedded in situations that look like nos. Jot down some nos you are currently experiencing. Next to each experience you listed, describe some opportunities those nos could present. Do you have the opportunity to create something new? Do you have the opportunity to be in a new environment? Does your no present an opportunity to build new connections? Does your no present an opportunity to grow spiritually or intellectually? Each no is embedded with a yes.

3. Sometimes a no to one thing is a yes to something better. Describe a time when you didn't get what you thought you wanted and needed, only to receive something better. How can these past experiences help prepare you for future nos?

10

THE NO OF AN ULTIMATE ENDING

On Friday, April 11, 1975, my dad went to the hospital for a colonoscopy. Back then, medical technology was not as it is now. Today that procedure involves having a tube inserted into your body with a small camera at the tip, and the doctor looks inside using a computer monitor. The entire procedure takes a couple of hours from preparation to release, and the procedure can take place in a doctor's office. But in 1975 my dad was admitted to the hospital for an overnight stay.

I went to visit Dad that Friday evening. He had completed the procedure without complication and was resting comfortably in his private room. I was somewhat concerned because he was in a private room without any heart monitors. He had experienced a mild heart attack when I was in the fifth grade, and I knew he had ongoing coronary issues, but he seemed so alert and confident that I didn't mention my trepidation to anyone. I was glad he was doing well. My dad was my best friend.

The next morning, I was scheduled to fly to Chicago to attend a significant fund-raising event for the organization for which I worked. I had decided to stop by the hospital to see my dad on the way to the airport since I would be gone for the better part of the following week. When I arrived at his hospital room, he was not in his bed. I assumed they had moved him to a different room. The truth was that the anesthesiologist had given my dad too much anesthesia, and it induced a heart attack causing his death.

They had moved him because he had died. He was only forty-seven years old, and I was twenty-three.

I immediately became the head of my family. My forty-four-year-old mother and eight-year-old sister became my responsibility. Whatever plans I had for my life had to be placed on hold as I responded to the needs of my family. My brother was a twenty-year-old college student who would need to finish college and grow into his future. He would not be available to help very much with my sister and mother. That would be my job.

Even though I had been in near-death situations during my brief lifetime, death took on a brand-new meaning for me on that day. Looking back over the long years since then, I would say death became the ultimate no life could say.

As much as I admire Mr. Blind Man's strength, his obedience, and his testimony, he lived as long as people live and then he died. This reality is true for everyone throughout history. When a dead body was thrown into the prophet Elisha's tomb and touched Elisha's bones, the dead man came back to life and stood up (see 2 Kings 13:21). But after a while he died again. King Hezekiah was so sick he was about to die. After he prayed for more time, God granted him a fifteen-year extension (see 2 Kings 20:1–6)—and then he died.

Jesus miraculously raised Lazarus from being dead after he had been buried four days (see John 11:38–44). After Lazarus came back to life, Jesus joined him and his sisters for dinner at their house in Bethany (see 12:1–3). But Lazarus ultimately died, as did his sisters, Mary and Martha. A young man named Eutychus died after he fell out of a window during a service where the apostle Paul was preaching. After Paul took his dead body into his arms, the young man came back to life (see Acts 20:7–10). But Eutychus ultimately died later also.

The point is that all history has proved the book of Hebrews correct in its assertion that all humans have an appointment with death (see 9:27). The earth would be utterly unmanageable if we had to navigate our way around and coexist with every person who ever lived. Death is inevitable, efficient, and intimidating all at the same time. Death is the ultimate experience of life saying no.

The power Jesus displayed in John 9 is designed to prove a larger point than His ability to bring sight to the physically blind. Mr. Blind Man defied so many of the circumstances that hinder many of us from entering new seasons of accomplishment and joy. By saying yes when his life said no, Mr. Blind Man revealed exemplary determination, and he revealed a strategy that can be replicated by those who are inspired by his story. After he received sight, his spiritual eyes were opened, and he recognized that Jesus was his way of preparing for the future no of death (see vv. 35–41). The roles were reversed! The religious leaders were now the blind, but Mr. Blind Man could now see! It all had to do with Jesus, who has the power to transform death's no into the yes of eternal life.

HANDLING LIFE'S ULTIMATE NO

I will never forget the night my dad died. His death said no to me in some straightforward ways. I had to immediately cancel my trip to Chicago. I had bought a brand-new suit for this special occasion, which I wore to the hospital that morning to show to my dad. He never got to see it. Moreover, I had to break the news to my eight-year-old sister. She had been the apple of my father's eye. He had always wanted a girl, and my brother and I knew that. After she was born, my dad spoiled her rotten. Telling her our dad had died was one of the most challenging talks I have ever given.

My mother was suddenly a forty-four-year-old widow who had never lived independently. She was nineteen when she married my dad and moved from her mother's house directly to my father's house. She had never balanced a checkbook, paid the family bills, negotiated the purchase of a car, or studied the details of Dad's insurance policies. For the immediate future, Mom needed to depend on me for all that.

I had commuted from New Jersey to Chicago on a regular basis for two years before my father's death. I was preparing to settle into my role as the newly appointed national coordinator of a civil rights organization by working from the national headquarters in Chicago. This was my dream job, and I had a bright future in my position. The death of my father changed all that, and I had to quit my job in order to help my mother. Regardless, I was determined to say yes even though death was saying no.

I was soon responsible for organizing all the funeral arrangements to present to my mother for her approval. That included meeting with the elders of our church and informing them that I, not they, would be in charge. After getting things organized and settled at my parents' home, I went back to my apartment to change my clothes and start writing my dad's obituary. I began making a list of all Dad's accomplishments—serving in the United States Army, working his way through college with three jobs, and starting programs for disadvantaged youth. He was a part-time pastor of a small church, a public school teacher, and an amateur vocalist who sang in the church choir. The facts I knew my father would want in his obituary were that he had accepted Jesus as his personal Savior and he would be living with Him forever in heaven.

When I wrote those words, I realized my father was better off dead than I was alive. I had been baptized when I was twelve years old and had started going to church again as a young adult. I had taken the first step into ministry in my church by becoming "licensed" to preach. I had been fighting for justice and using Scriptures as the basis for my speeches—but I had never made a connection with God the way my father had. I wasn't able to claim with certainty that I'd be going to heaven after my death.

For me Christianity had become a platform, a strategy, and a language, but not a lifestyle. My Christian belief system was limited to social advocacy on behalf of the politically downtrodden and economically oppressed, and it stopped short of personal salvation and spiritual redemption. I was embarrassed. While writing my dad's obituary, I realized I needed to be involved in a spiritual movement that was socially relevant. Instead, what I had accepted was a social movement that had a spiritual ring to it. I wasn't a bad person, but I was ill prepared for my father's death, much less my own.

Although there are different approaches to Christianity that gave me the right to call myself a Christian before that night, my understanding of Scripture, conversion, forgiveness, redemption, and salvation causes me to mark that day as the day I truly became a Christian. On that night I physically got on my knees and acknowledged I was personally separated from God—I was doing my will and not God's will even though I was doing good things. I wanted God to forgive me, and I wanted Jesus to live in me. During my revelation I promised God I would do the work of the kingdom of God for the rest of my life and my work for justice would have at its core my pursuit of righteousness.

The certainty of death confronted me with an astounding no, and my life began to blossom as a result of saying yes to Jesus.

The man who received his sight began preparing for his death by saying yes to his belief in Jesus. I started preparing for my own death by accepting God's plan for salvation through Jesus. But there are also practical aspects to preparing for life's ultimate no.

A week before my father went into the hospital, he took me to the bank to show me the contents of the safe-deposit box he and my mom maintained there. When we arrived at the bank, we went into a small private room where Dad sat me down and told me that he fully expected to have no difficulty with his upcoming hospital visit. However, as his oldest child and as a grown man, he wanted me to understand his business affairs, and he wanted me to be prepared if there was a problem. He was very specific with his instructions: "Your mother will be in no shape to do anything if something happens to me. So you will have to take charge." That was Monday evening, April 7, 1975. Dad was right. One week later I was back at the bank handling his business.

Although it was difficult emotionally, handling my dad's affairs was a piece of cake because he had everything so well organized. Not only had he listed the tasks that needed to be performed, but he also had them listed in the order they needed to be performed. He had every name of every person I needed to call, every company to which he owed money, every insurance policy he owned including the one that would pay the mortgage on the house in the event of his death. He outlined how many death certificates I would need to obtain, whom to notify at his job about his death, and even what time to get to the bank to withdraw money before they would learn about his death. Remember—he was forty-seven years old. This list plus the accompanying documents and his will made it like painting by numbers!

Unless time is entirely disrupted by eternity, we are all going to experience death. That is why I listed those who were brought back to life earlier in this chapter. They all died at some point. The fact is, we are all going to die. We would rather not think about it or talk about it. People say things like "when I pass on" or "if anything ever happens to me" or "when she made her transition." The very word *die* conjures discomfort in many people, so much that they won't even utter it.

The best way to say yes to the no of death is to prepare for it. How can we prepare for something that we are too afraid to name? This is not to suggest that everyone should have a detailed set of instructions as my dad prepared for me. As some of the young people in my church would say, he was a little "extra"! However, I must admit that having such an organized set of instructions and documents made our bereavement period much easier to manage.

To summarize my dad's list:

- a written, up-to-date will
- a list of bills and debts

- official insurance and loan documents
- names and phone numbers for accounts (today that would include email addresses, websites, and passwords)
- a checklist of tasks to be performed

These items should be in a location that is easily accessible and secure.

Another way to say yes to the no of death is to have enough life insurance to replace your financial provision for anyone who depends on you. When my dad died, he had enough insurance to leave my mother debt free. All the equity in their home belonged to her. She also had enough insurance money to trade in her old car and buy a new car with cash, thus eliminating a monthly car payment. To secure those financial provisions for my family, my dad and the entire family had to do without certain items while he was alive to pay the insurance premiums that kept these policies in force.

In my book *Say Yes to No Debt*, I describe a strategy that can help people figure out how to afford the kind of insurance they need. The dfree movement that began in 2005 has been encouraging people to secure the advice of certified financial professionals to create a plan for financial security in life and death. In my *Say Yes When Life Says No Workbook*, you will be given an opportunity to write down your life goals and consider your long-term financial goals in that process. Death is much less intimidating when we plan for its inevitable occurrence.

When I was diagnosed with cancer, I did the same thing with my sons that my dad had done with me. I took them to my bank and into a small private room where I showed them the contents of my safe-deposit box. I told them they were old enough to understand the family business since they were twenty-one years old. Before this visit my sons were visibly disturbed by the fact that I had cancer. They were very quiet, never wanted to talk about it, and weren't hugely interested in going with me to the bank. Even as we walked into the bank, it was apparent that this was not their favorite time with their dad.

I'm sure they will never admit this, but after they saw the assets we owned, the insurance policies we had, and the provisions we had in place for their mom and them, they left the bank a bit more encouraged than when they walked in. It was almost as if they were saying, "Well, Dad, we hope the best for you, and we'll be praying for you, but …!" Death and mourning are easier to handle when the deceased are prepared for that day.

Sufficient insurance is one crucial aspect of preparation. It is also essential to have a legal will. For a long time, I thought I didn't have enough money to justify having a will. When my children were minors, I learned I needed a will to determine where they would go should my wife and I die at the same time. Without such a will, the government would have made that decision about my children. Everything I owned would be subject to a government bureaucratic decision if I didn't have a will. A legal will is saying yes to the no of death because you retain your power to have important things happen after you die, and you deny death the last word in your life.

HAVE COURAGE

Saying yes to the no of death also means facing death with courage. At a recent funeral, a woman reported that she overheard her ninety-three-year-old mom telling her doctors not to resuscitate her should she die in their care. Her mom needed a machine to breathe. The woman said her mother sat up in bed, pointed at her and the doctor, and exclaimed, "You'd better not resuscitate me! I am ninety-three years old, and I am ready to go!" She faced death with courage. It's not as if a fear of death makes death optional, and facing death with courage makes life more meaningful while we live on earth.

One of the most challenging parts of retirement planning is having to state how long you want your retirement funds to last. If you want to retire at age seventy and you're trying to determine how much money you need to retire, the critical question you must answer is how long you plan to need your retirement funds. In other words, when do you plan to die? On one Sunday morning, after I had finished revising my retirement plan, I announced to my congregation when I planned to die. They were so shocked you would have thought I had announced a decision to commit suicide.

My congregation never gave me a chance to explain that I have a plan B just in case I don't die at that age. You can't take retirement seriously unless you give serious consideration to the length of your days. And when you do that, you have submitted to the reality that you are going to die, and you are looking at the face of death with courage. At some point you will be able to say as the apostle Paul said to his protégé Timothy, "I have fought the good fight, I have finished the race, I have kept the faith" (2 Tim. 4:7).

None of this is to suggest that we ever take death lightly or consider it a sign of weakness to grieve when experiencing the death of a loved one or a friend, or when facing death ourselves. One of the most frightening moments of my adult life was to watch a group of teens gathered around the casket of a young victim of gun violence and observe them interact as if they had gathered at an ice cream parlor. I was unnerved by how unmoved they were by the sight of their adolescent friend in a bronze-colored casket. But this scene was shaped by the fact that so many of their friends and relatives had been victims of senseless violence and their culture had glorified death and violence. They had become desensitized to the very sight and trauma of death.

There is a difference between courage and indifference. Even Jesus wept when His friend Lazarus died (see John 11:35). Facing death with courage does not mean we deny ourselves the right to express human emotions. It merely means we accept the ultimate reality that death will one day say no and we invest in strategies that will ensure we can say yes despite the pain we feel.

Finally, saying yes to the no of death means accepting the gift of life after death. This is what Mr. Blind Man accepted along with his sight, and this was more important than his eyesight.

By not believing that Jesus was who He said He was, the Pharisees could not see their ticket to life after death. They concluded that there was life after death, but they did not recognize Jesus as the means by which one obtained access to that life. So Jesus called them blind (see John 9:39).

I once traveled to Canada to speak at a youth rally that preceded a crusade Billy Graham was going to conduct. Whenever I worked at that kind of event, the event host would make a special effort to invite young people from diverse backgrounds and circumstances. This time they invited members of known gangs, hoping to convince them to follow Jesus.

While I was preparing backstage in a designated area, a staff member came to ask me whether I would speak to an actual gang leader. I agreed to meet this young man, so they took me to meet him behind the large curtain on the stage. When they led him over to me, he pulled out a knife and aimed it at my stomach. He said he had heard a lot about me and I was supposed to be a big-time speaker from the United States. "Let's see how big time you are when I stab you with this knife," he said. The Graham staff froze.

I said, "Young man, let me tell you two things. First, if you were to stab me with that knife, the worst thing that could happen to me is that I would die. And because I believe in Jesus and He is my personal Savior, I would go straight to heaven."

He looked amazed, then asked, "And what is the second thing you want to tell me?"

I answered, "I'm glad you asked. You're not going to stab me with that knife. I may be a preacher, and I work with Billy Graham—but I was born in Brooklyn, and before I would let you stab me, I would take that knife and shove it down your throat!"

When he heard those words and saw I was serious, he put away his knife and hugged me. He said, "I can listen to you speak because you are not a punk."

I certainly do not recommend that as a strategy for avoiding violent attacks! But I do recommend having a genuine belief in life after death you can describe with total certainty.

Someone once asked me how I could believe in heaven. I asked him how he could *not* believe in heaven. He said no one had ever come back from heaven to verify that it is real. I told him no one has ever been able to prove that heaven is not real. Those who do not believe in heaven or Jesus or the resurrection have had almost two thousand years to find the body of Jesus, and they have been unsuccessful. The disciples were divided and tortured after the resurrection of Jesus, and not one of them changed his story about having seen Jesus alive after He was buried in the tomb. The reason we can say yes in response to the no of death is that Jesus proved death does not have the final word when He rose from the grave alive on Easter Sunday morning.

Christians do not all agree on the details about heaven, but Christians should all agree that a loving God must have more for us than the no experiences that never stop coming in this life. Humans have perfected the art of killing other humans. People have devised rationales for oppressing other humans. Sickness and disease seem to be with us despite scientific discoveries, and death never goes away. When God disrupted all the chaos to create order, He had more in mind for people.

He had more in mind for us when He turned darkness inside out and forced it to coexist with light and when He summoned the wind and sprinkled the stars in the velvet sky. God had to have something tremendous in mind for us when He did the unthinkable and became one of us while remaining God. When He allowed the humans He made to nail Him to a tree He grew, to bury Him in the earth He created, then got up from the grave three days later, God revealed something big going on.

For us to be participants, not just spectators, all God requires is that we believe in and see His plan through the message and ministry of Jesus. When life says no, it can be impossible to see. It becomes possible when we ask God for the power and the vision to see our yes despite the obstacles that present us with a no.

TURNING YOUR NO INTO A YES

1. Reflect on your faith in Jesus. Is your Christian belief system a strategy you use, a language you speak, or your lifestyle? How can your belief system help you mentally prepare for life's ultimate no?

2. Think about the plans you have for your future. What promise will you make to God as you continue to live your life?

3. Make a list of items you have organized in preparation for life's ultimate no. Refer back to the list my dad left for me. What else do you need to do in order to help out those who will take care of matters after you pass away?

CONCLUSION

My in-depth relationship with John 9 and Mr. Blind Man was prompted by my prostate cancer diagnosis during one of the most successful and exciting years of my life. I believed I was doing everything a responsible patient should do. I attended all my scheduled appointments with the doctor and never allowed my busy schedule to be more important than my health.

I explored and considered all my options for treatment including having no treatment at all and just "riding it out" as some people describe that strategy. I did research on different doctors and health care facilitates to determine which was the best for treating my condition. I met with my immediate family and told them I had cancer and because the disease had been detected early, the prospects of my recovery were very positive. I met with the leaders of my church and made sure they heard the news directly from me and not from the talk around town.

We live in a relatively small community, and a larger than average number of families attend our church. My frequent visits to the Cancer Institute of New Jersey were certain to create at least a "buzz" around town. That was rather predictable when upon my first visit, one of the receptionists greeted me with a yell across the room. "Hey, Reverend Soaries!" I am known to show up in and around various local places, but no one keeps going to a cancer institute if not dealing with cancer.

I even informed my entire congregation on a Sunday morning and challenged our members to get checked for cancer. I urged them not to avoid an examination that could save their lives as mine likely would. I was busy doing everything I felt was the responsible thing to do. Yet deep down inside me, all I could think was that life had said no. And I felt it was unfair.

All my adult life I had worked on efforts designed to improve the lives of others. I had worked in communities to help low-income families improve the quality of their lives. I had led thousands of teens to accept Jesus as their personal Savior, and many of them were serving in ministries and churches around the world. I had been a pioneer in the contemporary gospel music industry, expanding the reach of urban gospel music. I had faithfully served in a church that had become a model for community development, financial literacy, foster care and adoption, outreach, and evangelism. I had never drawn a huge salary, a bonus of any size, or a 401(k) with a company match. I had enjoyed my accomplishments and my work.

But I couldn't believe God would allow someone like me to have cancer.

Have you ever felt as if God has ignored the fact that you have tried to be the best person you could be? Have you ever felt as if you were being mistreated despite your good deeds? As Christians we are not supposed to feel that way—especially Christian pastors. But not only did I feel as if God was actually saying no to me, I also felt bad for feeling that way. I never physically felt cancer in my body, but my mind and my emotions were in pain, because while I was comforting, advising, and motivating others to believe I was going to be all right, inside all I could hear was *no!*

No—you will never see your sons graduate from college. No—you will never see the affordable senior housing project completed. No—you will never see your next book released. No—you will not win this fight against cancer.

I wanted to find something to counter the negative thoughts of no that had begun to dominate my mind. I landed in John 9 because I was familiar with the fact that Jesus had performed a miraculous healing in this chapter. I needed the picture of Jesus' healing power to become more dominant in my head than the picture of cancer, sickness, and death.

I wanted the Bible to give me the assurance I had been giving to my family, my friends, and my church. I needed my faith to catch up with my words, because I was talking a good game but I was trembling on the inside. I needed an injection of belief that God could and would heal me. I wanted Jesus to do for me what He had done for Mr. Blind Man.

The outcome is what I have shared with you in this book. I was reassured that Jesus has more power than sickness—including cancer. And I was reminded that Jesus healed people who had never done anything for Him or the kingdom of God, so surely my faithful service made me eligible to be blessed with healing. But then the unexpected happened. Mr. Blind Man had a greater impact on my healing process than I could have ever imagined.

Ultimately, I ended up having a Christian surgeon use a robot to remove my prostate. I appreciated having a surgeon who prayed with me before the operation. The surgery was successful, the cancer had not spread beyond my prostate, and it has not returned. I am now cancer free.

But the real healing extends far beyond the cancer. I am under no illusion—the cancer did not kill me but something else will. I will not be here forever just because I am cancer free. The major healing I received was in what Mr. Blind Man did for my life. I arrived at some specific conclusions about the interaction between God's power and my responsibility when I attempted to deal with the nos in my life.

That is why I wrote this book. I am convinced that too often we bounce back and forth between thinking we can get past our no on our own (but giving up before really getting started) and getting desperate and running to God in an attempt to have divine deliverance and heavenly relief. I even have had people who don't believe in God or Jesus ask me to pray for them because their no is so incredible, they have concluded that only divine intervention can resolve their issue. This "Hail Mary" type of faith has a practical alternative that I hope has become evident in this book.

Allow me to summarize the list of things Mr. Blind Man taught me to do and not do:

- If you cannot see possibilities, don't assume they don't exist. Do take barriers seriously, but don't let them have the last word (see ch. 1).

- Don't allow yourself to be a prisoner of your present situation. Do use what you have in order to go beyond your situation (see ch. 1).

- Don't allow being alone to become loneliness. Don't miss the beauty and value of solitude. Do turn aloneness into solitude that brings peace and comfort (see ch. 2).

- Don't wait to be noticed, recognized, or accepted before proceeding toward your goal. Do have self-confidence that enables you to withstand criticism and rejection (see ch. 3).

- Don't let negative people push you away from Jesus. Do choose the people around you wisely (see ch. 4).

- When the worst happens, don't miss the possibility that the best is about to occur. Do remember that when you hit the bottom, there is no place to go but up (see ch. 5).

- Don't be afraid to find your solution in a place where solutions are not known to be found. Do remain willing to take the road less traveled (see ch. 6).
- Don't expect everyone to celebrate your success. Do expect those close to you to resent your success (see ch. 7).
- Don't underestimate the burden of victory. Do be prepared for the responsibilities that accompany things going your way (see ch. 8).
- Don't assume that everything appearing to be no is really no. Do look for the blessing in the mess and say yes to the circumstance that appears to be saying no (see ch. 9).
- Don't ignore the fact that life is temporary. Do prepare for the ultimate no and the ultimate yes (see ch. 10).

This not an exhaustive list. I am certain that if you study John 9 and spend quality time with Jesus and Mr. Blind Man, God will help you create your own list of life-changing discoveries. But I pray this content is useful as you develop your strategies for responding to the nos in your life with a resounding yes!

ACKNOWLEDGMENTS

It is through my writing and preaching that I share with others the insight I receive from God. I consider it a special privilege and honor to share with others, but I could not effectively do so without ongoing inspiration and support from many individuals. I thank God for those who help me positively affect the lives of people throughout the nation and world.

My most significant resource is Margaret Donna Soaries, my encourager, friend, and wife of thirty-three years. Her love, prayers, support, and critique are the most valuable assets I possess, and I am grateful to God for such an understanding and supportive partner.

This book is dedicated to the memory of my father and mother. I was raised by two parents who always demanded and demonstrated excellence in our home. My dad, DeForest B. Soaries, Sr., was a minister and English teacher. When I would ask my dad the correct spelling of a word, he would tell me to "look it up." At the time I did not understand that this was his way of forcing me to expand my vocabulary, think for myself, and become self-sufficient. Although I hated it at the time, he was my grammarian, and he insisted on proper English usage. My mom, Mary Soaries, also an educator, would stop my siblings and me mid-sentence if we spoke with improper grammar or word usage. Today I cringe at the normalization of nonstandard English in the media, and I am grateful for the educational foundation I received at home. I am deeply indebted to both of my parents, who prepared me for a livelihood that requires excellent communication skills.

Jen DaSilva worked with me on a couple of projects before this book. She is an extraordinarily talented educator who understands my style and knows my message. She worked her fingers to the bone making sure this book said what it was supposed to say. No writer could have a more reliable, committed person editing, proofreading, and completing his or her work. I hope Jen stays with me for a very long time. Special thanks to her.

I am also deeply indebted to Michelle Charles. I have developed a strategy that involves starting activities required for the next season while we are still in the current season. That makes for a very complex schedule and dynamic office environment. Michelle leads my hardworking, passionate, dedicated office staff and always ensures I make time to write.

I must express special thanks to the entire team at David C Cook. As a child I distinctly remember seeing their literature in our church. Never in my wildest dreams could I have imagined that I would have a relationship with this great ministry and a book published by them! Special thanks to Sharon Gilbert, Alice Crider, and Wendi Lord, who were responsible for consummating our relationship.

This book started as a series of messages titled How to Get to the Next Level delivered at First Baptist Church of Lincoln Gardens in Somerset, New Jersey. I owe a debt of gratitude to the leaders, notably the deacons and trustees, and members of our church for their support of my ministry and responsiveness to my preaching and teaching. Their support gave me the confidence I needed to expand my messages into books. Rev. Deborah Stapleton was the first leader to use a version of this material in an online Bible study. I am thankful for her teaching and her students' participation and feedback. My insecurity, as I wrote my first two books, was that no one would read them. I am indebted to the many people whose various responses to my previous books assured me that I really do have something to say and many are willing to read what I write.

This book focuses on John 9. The ability to extract so much value and content from one chapter of the Bible is attributable to the instruction I had as a religious studies major at Fordham University and a student at Princeton Theological Seminary. People often scoff at the notion that formal theological study is required for ministry. Unfortunately zeal and passion are not substitutes for training and knowledge. Dr. Byron Shafer, Dr. Bart Collopy, Dr. Clarice Martin, and Dr. Samuel D. Proctor guided my intellectual and theological formation that, of course, is still in process. I am eternally grateful for them.

Finally, I thank God for revealing in Scripture the encounter between the anonymous blind man and Jesus. This life-altering chapter of the Bible gave me just the perspective I needed to pursue personal, professional, and ecclesiastical integrity at a key juncture of my journey. My gratitude for the Bible requires that I express thanks not only to the Holy Spirit for the inspiration of Scripture but also to the writers, the interpreters, the translators, the defenders, and the publishers of the Word of God. My prayer is that the study of this chapter will motivate every reader to consistently use the Word of God to seek God's revelation for their lives.

NOTES

INTRODUCTION

1. Martin Luther King Jr., "I Have a Dream" (speech, March on Washington for Jobs and Freedom, Washington, DC, August 28, 1963).

CHAPTER 2

1. "Unabomber," FBI, accessed January 12, 2019, www.fbi.gov/history/famous -cases/unabomber; "Unabomber Arrested," History, updated August 21, 2018, www.history.com/this-day-in-history/unabomber-arrested; Stephanie Castellano, "The Moment the Unabomber's Identity Was Discovered," *Newseum*, September 1, 2017, www.newseum.org/2017 /09/01/the-moment-the-unabombers-identity-was-discovered.

CHAPTER 3

1. Coretta Scott King, foreword to *Strength to Love*, by Martin Luther King Jr. (Minneapolis, MN: Fortress, 1981), 9.

CHAPTER 6

1. James Weldon Johnson, "Lift Every Voice and Sing," in *Complete Poems*, ed. Sondra Kathryn Wilson (New York: Penguin Books, 2000), 110.

2. *Jewish Encyclopedia*, s.v. "Water-Drawing, Feast of," accessed January 15, 2019, www.jewishencyclopedia.com/articles/14794-water-drawing -feast-of.

CHAPTER 9

1. HomeVestors, accessed January 17, 2019, www.homevestors.com.

2. Steve Krakauer, "CNN's *Almighty Debt* Tops MSNBC's Maddow-O'Donnell Combination Thursday," *Mediaite*, October 22, 2010, www.mediaite.com/tv/cnns-almighty-debt-tops-msnbcs-maddow-odonnell-combination/.

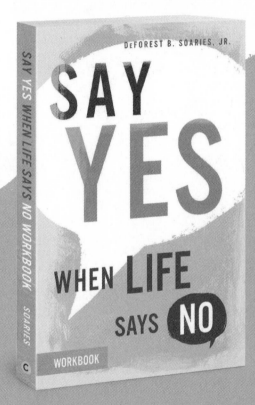